The Emotional Reset

OrangeBooks Publication

1st Floor, Rajhans Arcade, Mall Road, Kohka, Bhilai, Chhattisgarh 490020

Website:**www.orangebooks.in**

© Copyright, 2024, Author

All rights reserved. No part of this book may be reproduced, stored in a retrieval system, or transmitted, in any form by any means, electronic, mechanical, magnetic, optical, chemical, manual, photocopying, recording or otherwise, without the prior written consent of its writer.

First Edition, 2024
ISBN: 978-93-6554-895-2

The Emotional Reset

5R FRAMEWORK TO REWIRE NEGATIVE THOUGHT PATTERNS AND HEAL YOURSELF

DR. KETAKI PAWAR CHAVAN

OrangeBooks Publication
www.orangebooks.in

Dedication

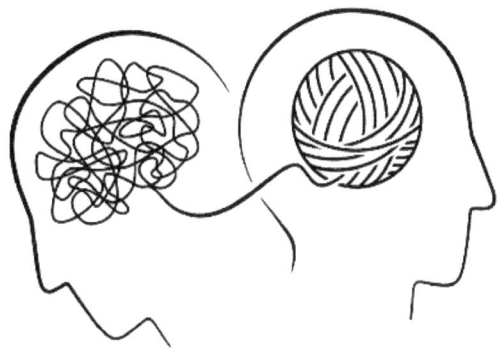

Dedicated to everyone struggling with their emotions

This book is for you— May it guide you on your journey to rediscover the strength within, heal from the wounds of the past, and unchain yourself to create a life of peace and fulfilment.

Foreword

As a licensed psychotherapist, I was trained to work with individuals with severe mental illnesses. I have also had the privilege of working with people who were simply unhappy or discontented with their lives or relationships. Each journey is unique, but there is clearly a need to help people deal with their emotions more effectively. It is with this understanding and a deep sense of admiration that I introduce "The Emotional Reset," written by my friend, Dr. Ketaki Pawar Chavan.

> *This book is more than a mere guide; it is a lifeline for anyone seeking to free themselves from the emotional scars of their past.*

Healing, as the book so poignantly states, is about reclaiming control and choosing to live a life filled with joy, purpose, and fulfilment.

What makes "The Emotional Reset" particularly powerful is its emphasis on active engagement. The exercises interwoven throughout its pages are based on solid psychology and mirror the stages of my own emotional work with clients, designed to challenge ingrained thought patterns and foster resilience. I often remind my clients that real transformation happens through action, and this book echoes that sentiment by encouraging readers to fully engage with its exercises.

I know how difficult this path of emotional healing can be. It requires courage, patience, and an unwavering commitment to oneself. But I have also seen the remarkable transformations that await those who persevere. "The Emotional Reset" serves as a gentle yet firm guide, encouraging readers to be patient and compassionate with themselves as they navigate this journey.

In closing, I encourage you to approach this book with an open heart and mind. Allow it to challenge you, change your thinking and habitual behaviours, and lead you toward a life where your past no longer holds power over you.

With warmth and encouragement,

Rick Cormier.

Psychotherapist,

Author of "Mixed Nuts or What I've Learned Practicing Psychotherapy"

Who Is This Book For?

This book is for anyone who feels trapped in a cycle of negative thinking, emotional overwhelm, or self-doubt and is ready to break free and create a more positive and resilient version of themselves.

If You Often Find Yourself Battling Negative Thoughts:

In **Step 1: Recognize**, you will learn to find the origin of your negative thoughts. If you've ever wondered why your mind seems to focus on the negative or why pursuing happiness pushes it further away, this step will help you recognize these patterns, offering practical tools to identify and challenge them.

If You're Curious About the Brain-Emotion Connection:

Step 2: Research is about studying yourself in depth as if you are the research specimen. You will understand how your brain processes emotions, what triggers them, and how to manage your triggers. We'll also explore how we can use the incredible power of our brain to transform itself (Neuroplasticity) for emotional healing.

If You Want to Transform Negative Thoughts into Positive Ones:

In **Step 3: Reframe**, you will understand how your thoughts shape your emotions and actions. This part is for you if you're not able to consistently practice positive habits like affirmations, gratitude, etc. You'll learn fun, effective, and extraordinary ways to add them to your daily routine, which will help you reframe your thoughts and start seeing the world—and yourself—through a more positive lens.

If You're Ready to Build Resilience and Inner Strength:

Step 4: Rebuild is dedicated to developing, mental toughness, resilience, and inner strength to face life's challenges with confidence. This step will help you build a toolkit of strategies for solving problems in life, finding meaning in difficult times, and strengthening your mind.

If You're Seeking Deeper Self-Love and Forgiveness:

Finally, **Step 5: Release** is about self-love, self-compassion, and forgiveness. It helps you understand the true meaning of self-love (It's not the same as self-care). If you've ever struggled with accepting your flaws, being kind to yourself when you make mistakes, or letting go of what doesn't serve you, this section will guide you towards a deeper, more compassionate relationship with yourself. True healing is possible only when you can release the past so that it no longer controls your present.

What is The Emotional Reset?

"Healing doesn't mean the damage never existed. It means the damage no longer controls our lives." — Akshay Dubey.

Emotions have the power to influence every decision you make, every relationship you have, and even your physical health. Like physical wounds, emotional wounds need attention, care, and time to heal. If left untreated, these wounds can cause deeper issues like chronic stress, anxiety, depression, strained relationships, and physical health problems.

You might be wondering, "Does everyone need to heal emotionally? What does it even mean? Does it mean we are all broken and need to heal ourselves?"

The truth is that everyone will need emotional healing at some point in their life, especially if they have been living their life to the fullest, going after challenges, and seeking growth.

So, it's not a shame if you need time to heal. It means you haven't been hiding from life but are facing it head-on. You're a warrior, and like all warriors, you may get injured and need time to heal, right?

Being human means experiencing a wide range of emotions, including joy, sadness, anger, and fear. It's normal to have emotional scars from life's experiences. Emotional healing becomes necessary when old memories or feelings still cause pain and impact your present. When we carry unresolved emotions, they shape our thoughts, decisions, and interactions with others, often in ways we don't even realize. Even if you generally feel okay, you can't reach your true potential in life until you let go of whatever has caused you emotional pain. We need to heal not just to fix what's broken inside us but to grow and become the best version of ourselves.

Gossiping is a bad habit, but have you ever noticed we often gossip about ourselves too? Not to others, but in the solitude of our own minds. We compare our lives with others, don't give enough credit to ourselves, and magnify our shortcomings. We tell ourselves, "Look, how easy their life is, and look at mine. Things never work out for me. I always have to work harder than others to get the same results. Nobody ever understands me. People are out to get me. If only I had the money to do that. If only I had their talent. I have always been like this, so what's the point?" … and so on.

This internal dialogue, this self-gossip, is destructive. It erodes our self-esteem, our confidence, and our happiness. It's time we recognize these negative thoughts for what they are: **Gossip**. Imagine overhearing someone talking about you in a negative manner. You would feel hurt, wouldn't you? Why do you think it's okay to hurt yourself by constantly painting yourself in a negative light?

And just like we would not tolerate someone else gossiping about us, we should not tolerate our own minds doing the same. We need to set this boundary with ourselves. Even if these thoughts are not harming anybody else, they are harming the most important person: **You**!

To overcome negative thoughts, we need to be aware of them and take proactive steps to focus more on the positive aspects of our lives. Sounds like common sense, doesn't it? Why is everyone not doing it? Why are people sad and depressed? They can just try to be more positive, right? I thought so too, and I wish it were that easy. But the human mind is complex. Even though we might know how to get ourselves out of our misery, what we need to do more than anything is to show more compassion towards ourselves when we go through tough times.

When you are under the spell of negative emotions, it's not easy to find happiness and motivation. People say there is light at the end of the tunnel but it's very difficult to see any damn light at the end of the tunnel when the tunnel is full of dense fog. This emotional fog can make it hard to believe in the possibility of better days, even though we intellectually know they exist. You could be surrounded by all the positive knowledge or books you will ever need in your lifetime but still not be able to grasp anything written in them because your mind is not receptive.

I have always been enthusiastic about positive thinking and self-help books. Over the past fifteen years, I have read hundreds of books on self-improvement, which has helped me a lot. However, during a certain challenging period of my life, negative thoughts started dominating my mind, and I felt overwhelmed by the weight of my emotions. I began devouring even more books, took courses in positive psychology, and watched countless videos on YouTube about managing emotions. I was on a quest to understand how the mind works and how I could control my emotions instead of letting them control me.

Well, little did I know that this path was not an instant fix. No matter how much I learned about managing my emotions, I would often fall back into the spiral of negative thoughts. Finally, I realized I didn't need more knowledge but more action. Things started changing only when I started creating practical exercises to apply the knowledge I had gained. I decided to make them simple, actionable, and practical. That's how I ended up creating a structured 5R framework that anyone can apply to get out of negativity, manage their emotions, and build resilience.

You already know how to overcome your problems. This book will help you get in tune with your inherent source of wisdom by using scientific strategies. However, don't try to think positively or try to be happy right away. You might say, "What kind of self-help book is this, telling me not to think positively? Aren't you going to tell me to meditate more, be more grateful, or think positive thoughts?" Nope, I'm not going to start the book with that because it's almost impossible to think positively when it is the last thing you want to do.

I get it because I've been there myself. This shared human experience is what makes life so beautiful. While we are all unique individuals with different circumstances, our core experiences and feelings are remarkably similar. The concept of "Everyone is you pushed out" suggests that when someone behaves in a way you don't like, it's important to understand that, in their circumstances, you might act the same way. If you had experienced their life, you would likely have made similar choices. *We act differently because we are shaped by different environments, but at the heart of who we are, we all share the same fundamental human experiences.*

This is why you and I feel the same emotions when we're hurt. The journey I've taken to become a better, happier, more confident version of myself applies to you as well. I understand what it's like to feel completely drained when all you want to do is lie in bed and cry. If that's where you are right now, it's okay—Don't be hard on yourself.

On this journey, you might start feeling better and think you have healed. But feeling better temporarily doesn't mean you have healed. If you burn your hand and the doctor gives you pain medicine, the pain will go away. But that doesn't mean you have healed, right? Healing requires patience. Growing from experiences and learning how to handle future challenges takes time. On some days you may feel worse than when you started the journey. But you need to be patient with yourself and keep going. The goal is to reach a stage where whatever has happened in the past no longer has control over you and where you are becoming a better version of yourself every day. So be patient with yourself and keep moving forward—you're building a foundation for lasting change.

How Does The Emotional Reset Work?

The Emotional Reset works through the 5R framework that guides you through the process of rewiring your emotional and mental patterns. Each step is designed to help you gradually move from a state of negativity and overwhelm to one of positivity and inner peace.

1. **Recognize** – The first step is about becoming aware of the negative thoughts and emotions that are holding you back. You can't change what you don't know. By recognizing these patterns, you begin to take the first step towards emotional freedom.

2. **Research** – In this step, you build the knowledge necessary to kick-start your healing process. You learn how your brain processes emotions, and how you can identify and manage your emotional triggers.

3. **Reframe** – Once you understand your emotions, it's time to change the way you think. Reframing is about looking at your situations differently, finding the silver linings, and replacing negative thoughts with more positive, constructive ones.

4. **Rebuild** – This step focuses on building resilience and inner strength. You will learn how to find meaning in suffering and turn your challenges into opportunities for growth.

5. **Release** – The final step is about letting go of what no longer serves you and learning to love yourself unconditionally. Whether it's past hurts, grudges, or limiting beliefs, releasing these allows you to move forward with a lighter heart and a clearer mind.

At any moment, you have the power to redirect your life. The key is knowing that you can hit the reset button right now—in the present moment. By regularly resetting your emotions, you can maintain mental and emotional well-being, leading to a life that's not only happier but also more meaningful and fulfilling. I am here with you every step of the way.

How to Read This Book

1. Read with an Open Mind and Heart

Some concepts might challenge your existing beliefs or feel uncomfortable at first. That's okay. Growth often requires us to step out of our comfort zones. Trust the process and be willing to explore new ideas and perspectives.

2. Take Your Time

This book is structured into five parts, each building on the previous one. Don't rush through them. Take your time with each chapter, allowing the ideas to sink in. You will need time to understand the science of your mind. Reflect on what you've read before moving on to the next section. The goal is not just to read but to absorb and apply the concepts to your life.

3. Engage Fully with the Exercises

Throughout the book, you'll find exercises designed to help you put the principles into practice. They are based on cognitive behaviour therapy. These exercises are where real transformation happens. I urge you to work on them. Don't skip them, even if they seem challenging or time-consuming. These exercises are crafted to guide you step by step through the process of emotional healing and resilience-building.

4. Journal Your Thoughts and Progress

Keep a journal as you work through the book. You might experience a storm of thoughts and emotions as you read and feel overwhelmed. So, it's a great idea to have a place to sort them out. Write down your thoughts, feelings, and any insights that arise. Journaling will help you track your progress and provide a space to process your emotions.

5. Practice Patience and Compassion

Change doesn't happen overnight. Be patient with yourself as you work through the exercises and concepts. There may be times when you feel stuck or frustrated—this is a natural part of the journey. Be kind to yourself and remember that every small step forward is progress.

6. Reach out if you need help

If you are stuck and need help understanding any of the steps, feel free to DM me on Instagram @drketakip or email me at drketaki.oms@gmail.com. I'll be happy to help you on your healing journey.

Contents

Dedication v
Foreword vi
Who Is This Book For? viii
What Is The Emotional Reset? x
How To Read This Book xv

Step - 1: RECOGNIZE
The Root Causes Of Negative Thoughts 1

Chapter - 1
Why We Focus On The Bad: Understanding Negativity Bias 2

Chapter - 2
The ~~Pursuit~~ Pressure Of Happiness: Why Trying To Be Happy Can Backfire ... 8

Chapter - 3
Where Do Negative Thoughts Come From? 16

Chapter - 4
Have You Trained Yourself To Be Helpless? 19

Chapter - 5
How Your Mind Plays Tricks You 22

Step - 2: RESEARCH
Understanding The Brain And Emotions 31

Chapter - 6
Why EQ Matters 32

Chapter - 7
What Sets You Off? Decoding Emotional Triggers 39

Chapter - 8
Taking Control Of Emotional Triggers 45

Chapter - 9
How Your Brain Processes Emotions 50

Chapter - 10
Reconnect With Happiness Using Your Hippocampus 58

Chapter - 11
The Power Of Neuroplasticity In Emotional Healing 63

Step - 3: REFRAME
Change The Way You Think 70

Chapter - 12
How Your Thoughts Shape Your Emotions And Actions 71

Chapter - 13
Changing The Narrative With Affirmations 79

Chapter - 14
Rewiring Your Brain With Gratitude 90

Chapter - 15
You Daily Emotional Detox 96

Step - 4: REBUILD
Build Resilience And Inner Strength 102

Chapter - 16
What Is Resilience? 103

Chapter - 17
Social Support: Your Key To Resilience 107

Chapter - 18
Trauma Can Be A Blessing 114

Chapter - 19
Use Pragmatism To Solve Problems 121

Chapter - 20
Resilience-Building Toolbox 128

Step - 5: RELEASE

Cultivate Self-Love And Forgiveness 133

Chapter - 21
Self-Care Can Soothe You; Self-Love Heals You 134

Chapter - 22
How To Love Yourself Truly, Deeply, And Madly 137

Chapter - 23
Self-Compassion: The Gentle Art Of Being Kind To Yourself 145

Chapter - 24
Is It Possible To Carry A Grudge And Not Be Aware Of It? 150

Begin Your Reset 160

About The Author 161

Bibliography 162

Step - 1
RECOGNIZE
The Root Causes Of Negative Thoughts

Welcome to the first step of your emotional reset.

Before you can start to rewire your negative thought, patterns and make lasting changes to your mindset, you need to understand the sources of those thoughts. In this section, we will learn why we tend to focus on the negative and how to identify the tricks your mind plays on you. We'll also explore how you may have trained yourself to feel more helpless than you are.

By the end of this section, you will understand yourself better, shift your negative thoughts to make room for more knowledge, and be ready to move to the next step.

Chapter - 1

Why We Focus On The Bad: Understanding Negativity Bias

"A single negative thought can put a person into a downward spiral. It takes a flood of positive thoughts to pull them out."
- Roy T. Bennett

You're hiking on a hill and suddenly sense something moving in the bushes. Your heart starts pounding in your chest, your mind starts imagining a wild animal and you start trembling with fear. Even though you don't know what's out there, you've already assumed that it's something that can harm you. Why do we react this way? Why do we assume the worst? The answer lies in the concept of the negativity bias.

Most of us tend to focus on negative things more than positive ones. Our brain is just wired that way and it's not necessarily a bad thing. It's a big reason why you and I are alive today because our ancestors wouldn't have survived if they didn't pay more attention to negative stimuli than positive ones. If they were overly positive and didn't consider the dangers around them while hanging out in the forests, most of them would have ended up in the stomach of a tiger by the end of the day. It's good for us that they didn't have many self-help and positivity books back then, right?

The negativity bias doesn't just affect adults. It starts from the time you were just a baby! Research has found that infants show stronger reactions to a person frowning at them versus a person smiling at them. It shows just how deeply rooted this bias is in our minds.

Also, studies have shown that the neurons in our brain are activated more when processing negative information. It means that your brain makes you dwell on negative experiences and thoughts more intensely. You must have experienced this: you get ten positive comments on your pictures but a single negative one can easily ruin your day. Why do news channels only focus on negative stories of crime, disasters, and scandals? Because they know people won't pay as much attention to positive news. You may be in a great relationship with an awesome partner, and they might do lots of nice things for you. But if they make one mistake, you might find yourself fixating on it and judging your entire relationship and their character based on that one mistake.

In today's times, where the chances of a tiger crashing your morning office meeting are very minimal, the negativity bias can do us more harm than good. That's why there are self-help books to remind and teach us how to be more positive. Let's explore some of the downsides of the negativity bias in today's age.

The Downsides of The Negativity Bias

1. Chronic Stress, Anxiety, And Depression:
The problem with the negativity bias is that it can contribute to mental health issues like anxiety and depression. It's a bias, after all. A bias is an unfair or unbalanced tendency or a prejudice against something. It can make you favour one thing over another without a solid reason. You can't trust this bias to make the right decisions for you because it distorts reality. You can think of it like wearing red-tinted glasses and complaining that the world is red. We should be aware of negative things but not focus on them to the extent that they will make us view the entire world in a negative light and make us a pessimist.

2. Relationship Problems:
If you only pointed out your partner's flaws and fixated on them, it's obvious that such a relationship will not survive for long. These days, people are quick to spot a potential partner's bad traits, popularly known as 'red flags.' While it's important to recognize legitimate concerns, hyperfocusing on these flaws without considering the full picture can blind you to the positive qualities your partner brings to the relationship. It's not just bad for them but for you too, because you're missing out on the good things they can do for you.

This applies to other relationships in your life as well. Every person you meet is going to have some flaws, including yourself. If you only focus on the negative qualities of people, you won't be able to form genuine friendships. If you want others to overlook your flaws and accept you as you are, you have to be willing to do the same for them.

3. Poor Decision-Making:

Negativity bias can make you judge the world unfairly and can influence your decisions as a result. It makes you focus only on the risks of doing something, turning you into an overly cautious person. Let's say you wanted to start a business. You will find hundreds of reasons why you shouldn't start a business. Did you know that around 80% of startups don't make it past their first five years? If I had focused on this one bit of information, I wouldn't have been able to start a business. So, I consciously chose to focus on the success stories of the business world to gather that courage. If you only focus on the negative information, it can prevent you from growing and learning new things. Even if you don't succeed, at least you will have gained valuable experience to start another business venture and increase your chances of making it big.

4. Physical Health Problems:

Focusing on negativity creates stress in your mind and body. If you let that stress accumulate in your mind for a long time, it will turn into chronic stress which can affect your physical health in many ways including weakened immunity, cardiovascular problems, unexplained aches and pains, gut health issues, and sleep disturbances.

When you are on autopilot, you don't recognize negative thoughts and how they impact your mental health. Over time, they can get deeply rooted in your mind and start to feel like they are a part of you. They don't just affect how you feel—they also start to dictate how you will react in a certain situation. For example, if you have a habit of underestimating yourself and thinking "I'm not good enough" or "Things never work out for me, I'm just unlucky", you will never go out of your comfort zone and do things that help you grow like starting a business, going for that interview, getting your book or your music album out there no matter how talented you may be.

> *While our minds are naturally inclined to focus on the negative, we hold the power to shift this tendency. The most important thing is to be aware of the negativity bias so that you can change your perspective when you start thinking negative thoughts.*

We need to see things from a balanced perspective. In Step 3, REFRAME, we will learn how we can change the way we look at our experiences and reshape our emotional responses. The journey from negativity to positivity isn't instantaneous, but each step we take in this direction makes a difference.

Practical exercise: Spot Your Negativity Bias

1. ***Reflect on Feedback:*** Think about the last time you received feedback at work or school. How much time did you spend thinking about the positive aspects versus the negative ones?

    A. I mostly focused on the positive feedback.

    B. I equally considered both positive and negative feedback.

    C. I fixated on the negative feedback more than the positive.

2. ***Reacting to Mistakes:*** When you make a mistake, how do you typically react?

    A. I acknowledge it, learn from it, and move on.

    B. I think about it briefly, but it doesn't affect me much.

    C. I dwell on it and worry about making the same mistake again.

3. ***First Impressions***: When meeting someone new, do you find yourself more focused on their positive qualities or their flaws?

    A. I notice and appreciate their positive traits first.

    B. I see both positive and negative qualities equally.

    C. I tend to notice flaws or potential issues before anything else.

4. ***Daily Reflections:*** At the end of the day, do you find yourself thinking more about what went well or what went wrong?

    A. I mostly think about the good things that happened.

    B. I think about both the good and bad equally.

    C. I focus more on what went wrong or what could have been better.

5. ***Social Interactions:*** After a social event, how do you typically feel?

    A. I feel good about the positive interactions I had.

    B. I think about both positive and awkward moments equally.

    C. I often worry about any awkward moments or things I say that might have been misunderstood.

Scoring:
- **Mostly A's:** You generally have a positive outlook and don't let negativity bias affect you much.
- **Mostly B's:** You have a balanced perspective, but there might be moments where negativity bias creeps in.
- **Mostly C's:** You tend to focus on the negative more than the positive, indicating a stronger negativity bias.

Results:
- **Mostly A's:** You have a positive mindset and are less likely to be influenced by negativity bias. Keep nurturing this attitude by practicing gratitude and focusing on positive experiences.
- **Mostly B's:** You have a good balance between positivity and negativity, but there's room to improve your outlook. Pay attention to when negativity creeps in and try to consciously redirect your focus towards the positive.

- **Mostly C's:** It's normal to have moments of focusing on the negative, but this exercise shows that your negativity bias might be influencing your thoughts more than you'd like. The good news is, the practical tools given in step 3 REFRAME, can help you train your mind to shift towards a more balanced and positive perspective.

Chapter - 2

The ~~Pursuit~~ Pressure of Happiness: Why Trying to Be Happy Can Backfire

"Those only are happy who have their minds fixed on some object other than their own happiness."
- John Stuart Mill.

The Happiness Paradox

If you pursue success at work, you will work hard and achieve it. If we apply the same logic to happiness, pursuing happiness should result in greater happiness, right? But it's not that straightforward.

Research says that over-emphasizing the pursuit of happiness or trying too hard to be happy can work against you and cause greater levels of unhappiness. We tend to set certain standards of happiness that are very difficult to obtain which is why we feel disappointed.
This is "The Happiness Paradox".

The more you want happiness, the more it runs away from you. Studies also point out that when a person has every reason to be happy but doesn't, he feels disappointed. For example, it's your birthday and you know that you have to be happy. It almost creates pressure on you to be happy. Naturally, you will feel unhappy because the pursuit of happiness has now become the pressure of happiness.

Like me, if you read a lot of self-help books, you may have felt this pressure too. Especially if you know about the law of attraction, you may feel guilty for thinking negative thoughts. The law of attraction says that negative thoughts attract more negative circumstances to you. But to reach that level of mental mastery where you can control your thoughts can take time and effort. It doesn't come naturally to many of us. So, this pressure to only have positive thoughts makes you judge yourself whenever you feel anything other than joy.

An Experiment on Happiness

Researchers conducted an interesting experiment in 2003. They formed two groups of people. They told the first group that they had to make themselves as happy as possible while they listened to a piece of music. They gave no instructions to the second group. Can you guess which group felt happier? Ironically, the first group reported feeling less happy than the second group. Where did the first group go wrong? They had the advantage of being instructed on what was expected of them. Well, that's where the problem started. This expectation created the pressure of being happy. As a result, they felt less happy. This research showed that chasing happiness does not necessarily increase happiness.

Prioritize Positivity, Not Happiness

How can you achieve happiness if you're not supposed to chase it? After all, that's what we want, right? You can be happy only when you release the burden of feeling happy all the time. When you let go of that pressure, happiness will naturally follow.

Instead of focusing on achieving happiness at all times, a more effective approach might be to prioritize positivity. In a study published in 2014, researchers explored the difference between individuals who prioritized happiness and those who prioritized positivity. Those who prioritized happiness agreed with statements like, "I am concerned about my happiness even when I feel happy," and "If I don't feel happy, maybe something is wrong with me." They also often viewed negative emotions as a sign of failure, agreeing with statements like, "I see myself as failing in life when feeling depressed or anxious."

In contrast, those who prioritized positivity focused on nurturing positive emotions in their daily lives. They agreed with statements such as, "I structure my day to maximize my positive experiences," and "I seek out opportunities that bring me joy."

The result was that people who prioritized happiness were more likely to struggle when they faced negative emotions. Those who were less fixated on chasing happiness and more interested in creating moments of positivity experienced more positive emotions.

It's important to normalize that it's okay to feel sad. It doesn't make you a failure in life. What matters is that you feel all your emotions and move through them instead of being stuck. Negative emotions are like the common cold. They need to run their course.

Prioritizing positivity means focusing on personal growth, nurturing positive habits, setting meaningful goals, practicing gratitude, exercising, and eating well. These actions are in your control which means nurturing positive emotions is also in your control. When you chase personal growth, happiness is the natural byproduct.

When I first read about the research on prioritizing positivity, it was a game-changer for me. I was struggling emotionally at the time. So, I decided to try it out without expecting much. I started looking for ways to add positivity to my daily life. Instead of overthinking I decided to fill most of my free time with activities I missed out on in my childhood. For example, I always wanted to learn to sing. So, I signed up for singing classes. It felt like scheduling happiness because I intentionally created positive moments in my life. One of the biggest benefits I experienced was that when I was fully engaged in positive activities like working out, reading a book, singing, or meditating—when I was in a state of flow—I didn't even think about happiness. I was simply enjoying the moment.

If you're struggling emotionally, instead of forcing yourself to be happy, fill your life with meaningful activities that you enjoy and create a state of flow. It will free your mind from unnecessary thinking and worrying, creating more space for positive emotions.

Happiness Set Point

While it may seem like your brain wants to focus on the negativity (The Negativity Bias), you can rewire it for positivity. You have more control over your happiness than you think. Each of us has a set level of happiness that doesn't depend on what happens in our lives. This is known as our

"Happiness Set Point". Even if you won the lottery today, it's not going to make you any happier in the future. Research on lottery winners showed that initially, winning the lottery made the winners very happy. However, over time, many lottery winners returned to their baseline level of happiness: their Happiness Set Point. This is called "hedonic adaptation." It means that people quickly get used to new circumstances, even when those circumstances involve vast wealth. As a result, the initial joy of winning fades, and winners often go back to their pre-lottery levels of happiness.

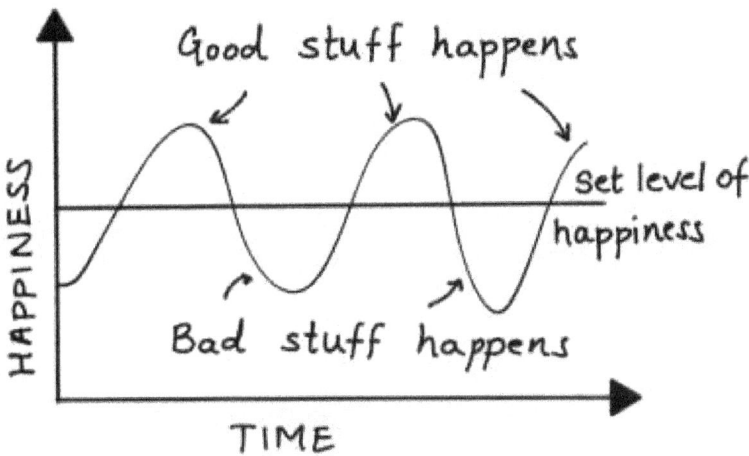

Now you may ask, "What controls this set point?" Take a look at the diagram of the Happiness Pie. Genetics account for approximately half of this set point. Yes, our happiness level is partly inherited! Only about 10% of our happiness comes from our life circumstances, such as our job, spouse, where we live, or how much money we earn. What about the rest? A whopping 40% of our happiness is determined by our actions, attitudes, and general outlook on life.

You might be wondering, "What if my happiness set point is genetically low? Am I always going to be unhappy?" Not necessarily! Remember, you still have 40% of your happiness within your control. It means that if you change your actions and your attitude, you can increase your happiness, no matter where your set point might be.

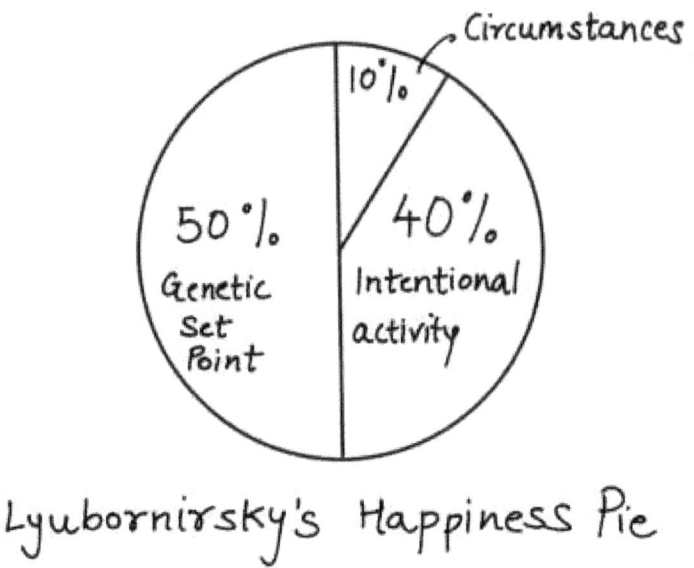

Lyubornirsky's Happiness Pie

You may not be able to completely avoid the negativity bias, but you can certainly train your mind to develop a more positive outlook. To achieve that, you need to learn the techniques to develop such an attitude and practice them wholeheartedly and consistently to be able to see results in your life. That's why it's called self-improvement or self-help.

No one can help you unless you take the responsibility to teach yourself and change your life for the better. As humans, learning is our superpower. When we don't know what to do, we learn how to do it. Nature has given us the mental faculties of learning, processing information, and taking action. We must use them to get out of misery, heal ourselves, and create our own beautiful destiny.

Don't worry. You are not alone in this journey. We're in this together. We'll explore how emotional healing works, learn about the brain's inner workings, and discover how to transform pain into personal growth. When you understand the impact of your thoughts on your emotions, you'll learn how important it is to replace these thoughts with more positive and constructive ones.

Carl Jung, a famous psychologist, once said, "I am not what happened to me, I am what I choose to become." I hope you choose to let go of your emotional baggage and become a stronger and wiser version of yourself. This is your chance to transform your challenges into opportunities for positive change. Absorb the knowledge I'm sharing with you and implement it in your life like your life depends on it—because it does.

Practical exercises:

1. The "Letting Go" Ritual
Objective:

To release the pressure of needing to be happy.

Instructions:

1. **Identify Pressures**

    Write down a list of pressures you feel related to being happy. Example:

    - "I must always be cheerful around others."
    - "I need to achieve this goal to be happy."

My List of Pressures:

- _____
- _____
- _____

2. **How These Pressures Impact Me:**

- _____
- _____
- _____

3. **Release the Pressure**

   Consciously decide to let go of each pressure. Choose a method to symbolically release them:

   - Tear up the paper
   - Burn the paper (safely)
   - Visualize them floating away like balloons

4. **Quiet Reflection**

   After completing the ritual, sit quietly for a few minutes. Focus on the feeling of lightness from letting go of these pressures.

How I Felt After Letting Go:

_____

_____

2. The "Enough" List
Objective:

To appreciate what you already have, reducing the pressure to strive for more happiness.

Instructions:

1. **Create Your "Enough" List**

   List things in your life that are already "enough" as they are. Example:

   - "I have enough love from my family."
   - "I do enough to take care of my health."

My List of "Enough" Things:

- _____
- _____
- _____

2. **Review the List**

   Whenever you feel pressure to pursue more happiness or perfection, review this list.

3. **Reflection**

   Reflect on how reviewing this list helps reduce your need to seek more or feel inadequate.

How Reviewing My List Made Me Feel:

_____

_____

3. Savouring Practice

Objective: To cultivate contentment by fully enjoying positive experiences without the pressure of them being "perfect."

Instructions:

1. Choose one small positive experience each day (e.g., drinking a cup of coffee, or walking in the park).

2. Focus all your attention on this experience. Notice the sights, sounds, smells, tastes, and feelings associated with it.

3. Allow yourself to fully enjoy the moment without thinking about how it could be better or worrying about when it will end.

4. After the experience, reflect on how it felt to simply enjoy the moment without the pressure to make it "happier" or "better." rewrite these in the form of worksheets.

In the next chapter, we will understand the role negative emotions play and explore practical strategies and tools for effective emotional regulation.

Chapter - 3

Where Do Negative Thoughts Come From?

"Your worst enemy cannot harm you as much as your own unguarded thoughts." – **Buddha.**

It's not the negative thoughts themselves that are the issue; it's when they become your regular way of thinking that the trouble starts. But how do these negative thought patterns even begin? Often, they start in childhood or teenage years. If a child is criticized often, he will grow up with self-doubt and negative beliefs about himself and the world.

I was always told that I was a shy kid, and it was considered a bad quality. People even pointed it out to my parents asking them why I was so quiet. I started feeling that something was seriously wrong with me. Like a self-fulfilling prophecy, I started avoiding anything that might draw attention. Over the years this belief got deeply rooted in my mind and created an identity of a shy person. Doing anything that would break that self-image was terrifying and out of the question for a long time.

Just like my belief about my shyness, you might be holding on to some other negative beliefs that started forming in your childhood. They might not be your true identity. Does that mean you blame your parents or other adults for your negative beliefs? Of course not! They made mistakes, just like everyone does. If they knew how impactful their words were, they wouldn't have said those things. Even if you think they did it out of spite, you can't blame them. Blaming others puts you in the mindset of a victim. As kids, we believe what adults say, but when we grow up, it's our job to rethink these beliefs. Are they true? Do they help us, or just hold us back?

To get hold of your negative thoughts, it's important to understand where they come from. Our brain is complex, and negative thoughts can arise from a variety of sources. Let's talk about some of them.

1. Evolutionary mechanism:

As we discussed in the first chapter, negative thoughts have deep evolutionary roots. Our ancestors needed to be aware of potential dangers to survive. So, they had to focus more on the negative aspects of their surroundings. Do these footprints look like they could be of a tiger? Does this cave look safe for me to live in and bring my girlfriend here? They had to overthink such things. In today's times, where most of us live in a concrete jungle and not a real one, this negativity bias often creates unnecessary stress in our lives.

2. Childhood Experiences:

Facing negative experiences during childhood, such as trauma, neglect, or criticism, can cause negative thought patterns. If we grow up around people who often criticize others, we may adopt similar thinking patterns. If you grew up in a household where your parents constantly complained about their jobs or said things like "Rich people are jerks" "Money is evil" or "It's a tough world out there," over time, you learn to view the world through a similar lens of negativity and doubt. As an adult, you might struggle to look at money positively, feel anxious about trying new things, or be overly critical of yourself and others.

3. Media and Environment:

Right after we wake up and start scrolling, we start consuming other people's thoughts. Most of the things we see online or read online are other people's beliefs about the world. Constant exposure to other people's beliefs can influence how we view ourselves and the world around us. For example, if you look at models with perfectly airbrushed bodies and flawless skin, you will start to feel like something is wrong with you. Research shows that more time on social media increases body comparison and negative feelings. It's not limited to women. Men also feel similar pressures to have muscular, lean bodies because of social media's unrealistic standards for attractiveness. When you see that the person in the mirror looks nothing like these standards, it can blow your confidence away and make you feel bad about your body even if you have a healthy body.

Social media often creates the illusion of a perfect life. Most people only post the highs of their life. They seem to go to the most beautiful vacation spots, have perfect relationships, live in huge houses, and be successful in their careers. When you start comparing your lows to their highs, negative thoughts are inevitable.

Many of your negative thoughts aren't facts but habits you've developed over time. Understanding where your negative thoughts come from is the first step to changing them.

Practical Exercise: Thought Tracker Exercise

Objective: To help you observe negative thoughts without judgment and prevent them from spiralling.

Instructions:

1. **Mindful Observation**: Spend 5 minutes each day sitting quietly, observing your thoughts. Don't try to change them—just notice them as they come and go.

2. **Record Your Thoughts**: After the mindfulness session, write down some of the thoughts you noticed, particularly the negative ones.
   - Example: "I noticed a thought that said I'm not good enough."

3. **Label the Thought**: Without judgment, label each thought (e.g., "self-doubt," "criticism," "worry").

4. **Practice Detachment**: Remind yourself that thoughts are not facts, they are just mental events. How does this realization change how you feel about the negative thoughts?

Source: Mindfulness-Based Stress Reduction (MBSR) techniques. Jon Kabat-Zinn's "Wherever You Go, There You Are".

Chapter - 4

Have You Trained Yourself To Be Helpless?

"Once you learn to quit, it becomes a habit." - **Vince Lombardi.**

Have you ever felt like no matter how much you try you will not succeed? After trying and failing multiple times, you may start to believe that there is nothing left to do and you are exhausted, both physically and emotionally. So, one day you just stop trying. Learned helplessness is that feeling of powerlessness that is a result of experiencing repeated failure. This idea was first discussed and developed by American psychologist Martin E.P. Seligman at the University of Pennsylvania in the late 1960s and '70s.

They were researching animal behaviour, and the experiment consisted of delivering electric shocks to dogs. Some dogs could escape the shock by pressing on a lever. The dogs who didn't have the option to escape eventually stopped trying to escape. Even when they could later escape by jumping over a barrier, they didn't bother to do so. Do you see what happened here? They learned to be helpless.

Similarly, if you keep facing failure, criticism, or negative experiences, you might start to think that nothing will ever improve, no matter what you do. When you think you have no control over your life, you might stop trying to change your life for the better, even when you have the resources to do so.

You need to make sure that you haven't given up on your dreams simply because you got tired of the effort to achieve them. It would be a huge waste of your infinite potential.

For example, you might have stopped working out because you don't see results after working out consistently for a few months. You might have stopped looking for a more satisfying job because you got rejected in interviews. That's learned helplessness. If you act out of learned helplessness, you don't fulfil your highest potential. To know if you may be a victim of learned helplessness, here is a practical exercise for you.

Self-Check-In exercise for identifying learned helplessness:

Step 1: Awareness: For each of these areas in your life, ask yourself specific questions like these and write in your journal.

Health: Have I stopped looking after my health? Have I given up on any of my health goals (e.g., weight loss, fitness, managing a condition)? Why?

Relationships: Have I stopped trying to improve my relationships? (family, friends, romantic) Why?

Career: Have I stopped trying to upgrade my career because of past failures or rejections? Why?

Personal Growth: Have I stopped learning and growing on my own? (e.g., learning new skills, education)? Why?

Finances: Have I given up on trying to earn more money because of past failures? Why?

Leisure and Hobbies: Have I stopped nurturing my hobbies or developing new ones? Why?

Step 2: Identify Patterns

Look for common patterns in your responses. Are there particular reasons or beliefs that keep coming up?

Identify any signs that show learned helplessness, like:

1. You have stopped trying to make things better because you believe that your efforts won't change anything.

2. You feel worthless and powerless because of repeated failure.

3. You feel trapped in your situation.

4. You avoid new situations or challenges to avoid more failure.

This is how you can pinpoint which areas of your life are affected by learned helplessness. If you have done this exercise, you can see how learned helplessness makes you stuck in one place. Identifying these areas is necessary if you want to progress in your life. In the next chapter, you'll learn to recognize all the tricks your mind plays on you to make you think negatively.

Chapter - 5
How Your Mind Plays Tricks You

*"Cognitive distortions are the shadows that obscure the light of truth from our minds." – **Unknown.***

You might think you already know how to spot your negative thoughts but it's trickier than you think. You might not even realize you have a negative thought pattern until something happens that triggers you and you respond negatively.

The way you think about things affects how you feel about them. You can sometimes make mistakes while thinking. These mistakes are called **Cognitive Distortions.** Cognitive distortions are irrational thought patterns that can make you think negatively. Such distortions are like those funny mirrors that reflect a skewed version of you. They make the situation seem worse than it is.

Have you noticed how hard it can be to shake off sadness once it sets in? That's because cognitive distortions make us feel trapped in our problems, convincing us that we can't overcome them.

I know it's a tough job to recognize these thoughts. That's why I am going to make it easy for you to understand and categorize your thoughts. Let's look at some common cognitive distortions you might have experienced so you can start to recognize and challenge them in your own life.

1. Catastrophizing

Do you turn small problems into massive disasters in your mind? For example, if you make a mistake at work, you might think, "I'm going to get fired and never find another job." If you face a breakup, you might think, "I'll never find love again." This is catastrophizing. Needless to say, this kind of thinking can leave you feeling anxious and overwhelmed.

2. Black-and-White Thinking

This is all-or-nothing thinking where you see things in extremes, with no middle ground. You might think, "If I'm not perfect, I'm a total failure." This kind of thinking doesn't allow for the many shades of grey that exist in life. Most situations fall somewhere in between, but black-and-white thinking can blind us to that reality. Think of it like cricket. Just because you got out on a duck once doesn't mean you're the worst batsman ever. Even the best players have their off days. Life isn't always about hitting sixes or getting bowled out; sometimes, it's about those singles and twos.

3. Overgeneralization

Overgeneralization is when you make a broad conclusion based on a single event. Suppose you have an argument with a friend and think, "I'm terrible at maintaining friendships. No one likes me." This is overgeneralization at play, as you're letting one disagreement overshadow all the positive interactions you've ever had. It's taking one instance and applying it to all situations, which can make you feel defeated and hopeless. One way to overcome this is to use realistic language. Instead of saying, "It always happens," say something like, "It happens sometimes."

4. Personalization

Personalization means taking responsibility for something that is out of your control. Sometimes when you make a mistake, it's not your fault and outside factors may be at play. For example, if you shot an arrow, and it didn't hit the target because of a forceful blow of the wind, would you still blame yourself? If you did, that would be a mistake in the way you think.

Let's say you organized a team meeting at work, and during the meeting, your manager seemed distracted and uninterested. You might immediately think, "I must have done a poor job planning this meeting." Your manager's distraction could be due to personal issues or a heavy workload, completely unrelated to your efforts. By personalizing their behaviour, you unnecessarily blame yourself, affecting your confidence and causing stress.

Parents often make this thinking mistake when they blame themselves for everything bad that happens in their child's life. For example, there could be a lot of reasons why the child performed poorly on a test. But parents tend to think it was entirely their fault.

Know that you don't control everything. It can help you avoid unnecessary self-blame and maintain a healthier perspective.

5. Mental Filtering

Mental filtering is when you focus only on the negative aspects of a situation while ignoring the positive ones. It's like getting ten compliments and one piece of constructive criticism but dwelling only on the criticism. Journaling is a great way to take a look at a situation from all sides. When you write about your day's events, you get to mentally revise how your day went. It helps you develop a neutral perspective instead of a negative one.

6. "Should" Statements

Should" statements are those rigid expectations you hold for yourself or others. Imagine you're working on a project and think, "I should never make mistakes at work." This expectation sets an unachievable standard, as everyone makes mistakes from time to time. When you inevitably make a small error, you might feel unnecessarily stressed or frustrated, thinking you've failed to meet your own expectations. Instead, recognizing that making mistakes is part of learning and growth can help you approach your work with a healthier mindset.

Another common "should" statement involves relationships: "My partner should always understand how I feel." While it's natural to want an understanding partner, expecting them to always know your emotions without communication can lead to misunderstandings and disappointment. Open and honest communication is always better to prevent unnecessary drama.

7. Emotional Reasoning

Emotional reasoning is when you believe something is true just because you feel it. Your gut feeling does not always guide you accurately. Just because you feel a certain way does not always mean it's true. Emotions are often the result of thoughts, and sometimes those thoughts can be wrong—this is what's known as *cognitive distortions*.

For example, you might think, "I feel anxious, so something bad must be about to happen." But those anxious feelings are likely coming from negative thoughts you're having, not necessarily from any real threat. Similarly, emotions like sadness can trick you into thinking, "I feel sad, so my life must be terrible." In reality, that sadness might be the result of a temporary situation, like a tough day at work or a minor setback. Just because you feel sad at this moment doesn't mean your entire life has been filled with sadness.

Emotions are powerful, but they aren't always reliable indicators of reality. It's important to recognize this so you can avoid letting your feelings control your thinking.

In the context of broken relationships, you might think, "I should get back with my ex because I miss them." But this feeling of missing someone doesn't necessarily mean the relationship was right for you, or that things will be different if you try again. You may miss them because you feel lonely, but there were solid reasons why the relationship ended, right? Otherwise, you would still be together. Loneliness can make you long for the familiar, even if the relationship was unhealthy or didn't meet your needs. So, remember, emotions are temporary and often situational. You must avoid making sweeping judgements about your overall well-being based on temporary feelings.

8. Labelling

Labelling involves assigning a fixed label to yourself or others based on one incident or behaviour. If you make a mistake, you might think, "I'm such an idiot." This kind of thinking turns a complex person into a single, negative quality. Let's say you and your partner are planning a vacation, and they forget to book the hotel on time resulting in your favourite spot being fully booked. In frustration, you might think, "They're so unreliable." This label ignores all those times your partner has been dependable and well-organized in planning other aspects of your life together. You focused on this one incident and reduced their entire character to a single negative trait.

9. Magnification and Minimization

Most of the time we tend to exaggerate negative events and minimize the importance of positive ones. For example, you might blow a minor setback out of proportion and downplay your successes. For example, failing a test and thinking it's the end of the world, or winning a small prize and thinking, "It's nothing, I just got lucky."

Imagine you give a presentation at work and make one small mistake. You might magnify this error, thinking, "Everyone must think I'm a loser now," even though the rest of your presentation was excellent. This magnification of the negative can overshadow all the successful aspects of your presentation.

On the flip side, think about when you receive praise for a project you completed. You might minimize this positive feedback by thinking, "They're just being nice," or, "It wasn't a big deal; anyone could have done it." You might think you're just being humble. However, minimizing your achievements and preventing yourself from fully appreciating your successes can lower your self-esteem and motivation.

10. Jumping to Conclusions

Jumping to conclusions means making negative assumptions without evidence. There are two common forms of this: mind-reading (assuming you know what others are thinking) and fortune-telling (predicting a negative outcome).

Mind Reading: If you text your partner and they don't respond right away, you might jump to the conclusion, "They must be upset with me," or "They just don't care about me," even though they might simply be busy or haven't seen the message yet. This assumption can make you feel anxious and react defensively when there's no real issue.

Fortune Telling: Suppose you're planning a date night, and things have been a bit stressful lately. You might think, "This date is going to be a disaster," before it even starts. This negative prediction can affect your behaviour creating a self-fulfilling prophecy. You won't fully open yourself up and talk to your date which will naturally result in a bad experience.

You may wonder why you need to know all these terms. I know you are not taking Psychology classes. But recognizing cognitive distortions is important because these distorted thinking patterns can significantly impact your mental health. When you identify them, you can challenge these negative thoughts. This process helps break the cycle of negativity. These thoughts can feel overwhelming, but remember, they're just that—thoughts, not facts. So, you can't rely on them. You just have to be aware of them so that they don't affect your judgement.

Practical exercise: Thought Transformer Exercise
Step 1: Identify the Negative Thought
Think about a recent situation where you felt upset or stressed. Write down the situation and the negative thoughts you had.

Example:
- **Situation:** I argued with a friend.
- **Negative Thought:** "I'm a terrible friend, and they'll never want to talk to me again."

Step 2: Spot the Distortion
Match your negative thought with one of these common thinking mistakes:

Distortion	Definition
Catastrophizing	Making a small problem into a big disaster.
Black-and-White Thinking	Seeing things in extremes with no middle ground.
Overgeneralization	Thinking one bad event means everything is bad.
Personalization	Blaming yourself for things you can't control.
Mental Filtering	Only seeing the negative and ignoring the positive.
Should Statements	Having rigid expectations for yourself or others.
Emotional Reasoning	Believing something is true just because you feel it.
Labelling	Giving yourself or others a negative label based on one event.
Magnification	Blowing negative things out of proportion.
Minimization	Downplaying positive events.
Jumping to Conclusions	Assuming the worst without evidence.

The distortion in this example is **Overgeneralization.**

Step 3: Challenge the Thought

Ask yourself these questions to challenge your negative thoughts:

1. **Evidence:** What facts support or go against this thought?

2. **Alternatives:** Are there other ways to look at this?

3. **Realistic Outcome:** What's the most likely outcome?

Example:

- **Evidence:** We've had arguments before and remained friends.

- **Alternatives:** Everyone has disagreements sometimes. It doesn't mean the friendship is over.
- **Realistic Outcome:** We'll likely talk it out and move past it.

Step 4: Reframe the Thought

Rewrite your negative thoughts in a more balanced way.

Example:

- **Original Thought:** "I'm a terrible friend, and they'll never want to talk to me again."
- **Balanced Thought:** "We argued, but we can resolve it like we have before."

Thought Transformer Template

Step	Action	Your Response
Step 1	Identify the Negative Thought	
Step 2	Spot the Distortion	
Step 3	Challenge the Thought	
Step 4	Reframe the Thought	

Tips for Practice:

- Write down situations where you feel negative.
- Use this worksheet to challenge and reframe your thoughts regularly.

These steps can be applied to various aspects of personal transformation, from developing new skills to improving your emotional well-being.

Now that you know better, you can spot and change these negative thought patterns. If you don't, these thoughts can lead to anxiety, low self-esteem, stress, and even trouble in relationships. They can also cause a plethora of physical issues from cardiovascular problems to headaches or gut health problems.

Overcoming cognitive distortions doesn't mean you have to eliminate negative thoughts completely. You just have to see them for what they are and respond to them in a healthier way.

Now that you've completed Step 1 and learned how to identify and understand your negative thoughts, you might be excited for the next step. In the next chapter, we'll discuss how our thoughts, emotions, and behaviours influence each other and how you can use this knowledge to shift your thoughts and improve your life. However, I urge you to complete the practical exercises of Step 1 first so that you will understand yourself better and pinpoint exactly what is holding you back and how to let it go.

Step - 2
RESEARCH
Understanding the Brain and Emotions

This step is called "Research" because you will study yourself like a research specimen and learn how to manage your emotions through scientific knowledge. We will begin with understanding the role of negative emotions, decode your emotional triggers, and learn how to manage them effectively so that they no longer have the power to influence you. Then we'll understand how our brain works and processes emotions, the incredible power of neuroplasticity, and how you can harness it for your emotional well-being.

Chapter - 6
Why EQ Matters

*"The emotion that can break your heart is sometimes the very one that heals it." – **Nicholas Sparks***

In a quiet village at the edge of a dense forest, there lived a wise monk. The villagers respected him deeply for his serenity and wisdom. One day, a young and impatient warrior named Jack arrived in search of the monk's wisdom.

"Master," Jack said, his voice tense with frustration, "I am constantly losing control of my temper. It hinders my progress and brings me shame. How can I master my emotions?"

The monk nodded thoughtfully and handed him a small, smooth stone. "Take this stone to the river and place it in the flowing water," he instructed. "Then, return to me."

Puzzled, Jack did as he was told. When he returned, the monk asked, "What happened to the stone?"

"The water flowed around it," Jack replied. "The stone remained still while the river rushed by."

The monk smiled gently. "Our emotions are like the river—ever-changing and often turbulent. But we can choose to be like the stone, grounded and unmoved by the flow."

Every day, we experience a wide range of emotions—joy, sadness, anger, fear, and everything in between. They rule most of the decisions we make. You must have experienced that you may have the best intentions, but you are unable to translate them into action. For example, you decided to go to the gym every day starting 1st of January but you couldn't follow through and reach your fitness goals. Why? Because most days you didn't "feel" like going to the gym. When you made the resolution, you didn't consider the emotions that could impact you. You may not be aware of this, but your emotions influence your decisions, and some of these decisions could sabotage your long-term happiness.

Let me give you another example. Let's say you've broken up with someone and decided not to contact them again or respond to their texts. The healthy choice would be to stick to your decision. But then something reminds you of them, and you start feeling nostalgic, so you send them a text. Deep down, you know it's not in your best interest, and you probably shouldn't have contacted them. You've even given similar advice to a friend who was going through a breakup. Yet, despite knowing better, you struggle to manage your own emotions and keep falling into the same pattern, which only ends up delaying your healing process. Like these, there are other reasons why it's so important to learn to manage your emotions effectively.

Importance of Managing Emotions Effectively

1. *Impact on Mental and Physical Health:* When we don't know how to handle stress and negative emotions, it can lead to anxiety, depression, and even physical health problems like high blood pressure. But when we learn to manage our emotions effectively, we can start thinking clearly and become more peaceful.

2. *Role in Relationships:* Managing our emotions helps us communicate better which helps resolve conflicts. When you know how to handle your emotions, it puts less pressure on your partner to make you happy and creates less drama in the relationship. It also makes room for your partner to be more open and honest with you when they know you won't react immediately or dramatically.

3. *Personal Growth:* What you achieve in life is deeply connected to how you manage your emotions. When you educate your emotions to work with you and not against you, you will find it easy to stay disciplined. Learning new things and reaching your goals is easier when you are emotionally stable.

So, what should you do to avoid getting influenced by your emotions and stick to your decisions? You need to improve your ability to recognize, understand, and manage your emotions. It's also known as EQ or Emotional Intelligence. It doesn't mean you need to suppress your feelings. It simply means understanding the messages your emotions are trying to convey and navigating through them in a way that serves your highest good.

Why Negative Emotions Matter

You may be surprised to know that negative emotions like sadness, anger, and fear also have a role to play. They aren't all bad and if you experience them, it doesn't make you a bad person either. Several studies have shown that experiencing both positive and negative emotions is beneficial for your well-being because it shows that you have good emotional clarity.

In a world that is obsessed with being happy, we are told that if you experience negative emotions, it means there's some problem with you that must be fixed immediately. So, instead of dealing with the issues that make us feel these emotions, we look for instant solutions to be happy because we want to fit in the world. We confuse pleasure with happiness and get sucked into bad habits.

Instead of labelling your emotions as purely negative, think of them as messengers with important messages to share. If you look at them this way, they can help you understand yourself better and identify areas where you can grow. For example, if you find yourself feeling angry after something your partner says, that anger isn't necessarily a bad thing. This emotion is trying to tell you that something is bothering you, and both of you need to work on it. You may need to set boundaries or discuss a problem that affects both of you.

Here's a simple table to help you understand what your negative emotions are trying to tell you.

Negative Emotion	Hidden Message
Anger	Anger is unprocessed trauma trying to make itself known to you so that you will finally start working on your triggers. It tells you to go within and work on the root cause of your anger. It could be a sign that you need to stand up for yourself or set better boundaries.
Sadness	Indicates a loss or unmet need, urging you to reflect, grieve, or ask for help. It tells you to accept the unpredictable nature of circumstances and go with the flow instead of resisting what's happening. Sadness also helps you connect with other people by allowing them to recognize that you need extra emotional support.
Fear	Can indicate self-doubt and inner conflict. You might be avoiding something that threatens to push you out of your comfort zone. It could be telling you to face your fears and grow from the experience.
Guilt	It tells you that you have set unrealistic standards of perfection for yourself and that you need to be kind to yourself. It also shows that your actions don't match your values. You may need to change your actions or adjust your values.
Shame	You might be accepting others' judgments. It could be a reminder to accept yourself and challenge negative beliefs about yourself.
Frustration	This could indicate that you're not recognizing your progress. It might be telling you to celebrate small accomplishments and adjust your expectations.
Jealousy	You might be feeling insecure about your own worth. It could be a signal to build self-confidence and

	appreciate your unique qualities. It also helps you to know what you truly want and how to achieve it by studying the people you're jealous of.
Loneliness	This could be a sign that you're not taking care of your relationships. It might be telling you to reach out and reconnect with loved ones. It also tells you to learn to enjoy your own company.
Anxiety	It shows that you are believing everything your mind is telling you. You might be overestimating problems and underestimating your ability to solve them. It could be a signal to build resilience and trust in your capabilities.
Disgust	This could indicate a deeper moral or ethical conflict. It might be telling you to reflect on your values and make choices that align with them.

If you haven't already watched "Inside Out," I highly recommend it. The film brilliantly shows that all emotions are important, even the ones we often label as negative, like sadness. In the movie, we see emotions like Joy, Sadness, Fear, Anger, and Disgust—all personified as characters in young Riley's mind—each playing a vital role in her life.

As Riley goes through significant changes, like moving to a new city and leaving behind her familiar life, her emotions are all over the place. Initially, Joy tries to keep everything positive, believing that Riley should always be happy. But as the story unfolds, it becomes clear that this isn't sustainable. When Joy doesn't allow Sadness to be expressed, Riley becomes emotionally numb and unable to function normally. Finally, Joy lets go of the pressure to make Riley feel happy and allows Sadness to take the lead. As soon as the emotion of sadness is allowed back into Riley's mind, she immediately comes back to her senses. She stops pretending that everything is fine, tearfully hugs her parents, and lets them know how she is really feeling after moving to the new place. Sadness helps her understand her feelings and reconnect with her parents.

In our lives, we often try to push away or ignore emotions like sadness, anger, or fear, thinking they are bad or counterproductive. But these emotions are not just inevitable—they're essential. They guide us through difficult times, helping us understand what we need and how we can grow. Instead of bottling up our feelings or pretending they don't exist, we can learn to process them in a healthy way.

So, if you haven't seen "Inside Out," give it a watch. It might just change the way you think about your own emotions.

Practical exercises:

1. *Constructive Conversations*

Purpose: To express and explore your emotions with others.

Instructions: Choose someone you trust and share an emotion you've been struggling with. Use "I feel" statements to describe your experience. For example, "I feel frustrated when I'm not heard in meetings because it makes me feel undervalued" or "I feel that I am not important to you when you forget the meaningful moments we spent together." Invite the other person to share their perspective and discuss how you can address the issue together.

2. *Quiz: Decode Your Negative Emotions!*

2.1 Which of the following is a common role of negative emotions?

a) To cause discomfort and disrupt our lives

b) To signal unmet needs or important boundaries

c) To keep us from achieving happiness

d) To encourage us to ignore our feelings

2.2 True or False:

Negative emotions should always be suppressed to maintain a positive mindset.

- True
- False

2.3 Which emotion might indicate that your boundaries have been crossed?

a) Sadness

b) Anger

c) Guilt

d) Anxiety

2.4 Describe a recent situation where you felt a strong negative emotion. What do you think this emotion was trying to tell you?

2.5 What is one constructive way to respond to negative emotions?

a) Distract yourself with a fun activity

b) Acknowledge the emotion and explore its message

c) Ignore it until it fades away

d) Let it dictate your actions immediately

Answer Key:

2.1 b) To signal unmet needs or important boundaries

2.2 False

2.3 b) Anger

2.4 Personal reflection (Answers will vary)

2.5 b) Acknowledge the emotion and explore its message

Chapter - 7

What Sets You Off? Decoding Emotional Triggers

*"Our emotions need to be as educated as our intellect. It is important to know how to feel, how to respond, and how to let life in so that it can touch you." - **Jim Rohn.***

Understanding What Triggers Your Emotions

Emotional triggers are specific stimuli—like people, situations, or events—that provoke an intense emotional reaction. These reactions can range from anger, sadness, and anxiety to frustration. Triggers can be external (from the environment) or internal (from personal thoughts and memories).

You need to be aware of what triggers your emotions if you want to free yourself from them. You can't keep nurturing your triggers and letting them affect your peace of mind. Triggers don't come with a warning, but they ruin our days and in turn, our life. You want to be in a position where your emotional responses are controlled by you, not your triggers.

Self-awareness is key to managing emotional triggers. By understanding what sets off your emotional responses, you can start managing them in a better way. Here are some steps to help you recognize your triggers:

1. Pay Attention to Your Reactions

Start by noticing when you have an intense emotional reaction to something. These reactions can be strong feelings of anger, sadness, anxiety, or even joy. Pay close attention to what happened just before you felt this way. You have to step into the role of the observer. For example, if you felt a surge of anxiety after receiving a phone call, consider what was discussed or who was on the line. Keeping track of these moments can help you identify specific triggers.

2. *Journal Your Emotions*

Writing down your thoughts and feelings can be incredibly insightful as well as liberating. Keep a journal where you note the times you felt a strong emotional response. Include details about what happened, how you felt, and any physical sensations you experienced. Over time, you may start to see patterns appearing. This can help you understand what consistently triggers certain emotions. For instance, you might notice that you often feel stressed after talking to someone, indicating that these situations are a trigger for you.

3. *Ask Your Network*

Sometimes, others can see our triggers more clearly than we can. Trusted friends or family members might notice things you haven't, such as specific situations that consistently upset you or behaviours that indicate you're feeling triggered. We often hate to accept that we were triggered. So, external input can help you understand and manage your emotional triggers.

The Role of Past Experiences and Conditioning

Our early years form the blueprint for how we look at life, acting as a lens through which we view the world. It's why some of us may struggle with fear, anxiety, or self-doubt, while others may approach challenges with confidence and resilience.

Research, like the groundbreaking Adverse Childhood Experiences (ACE) Study, reveals just how powerful these early experiences are. The study found that individuals who faced trauma in their childhood were more likely to go through mental and physical health issues later in life. Many of our emotional triggers come from unresolved issues or past experiences. Revisiting these memories can be painful but they can help us find out the root causes of our current emotional responses. For example, if you have a fear of failure, tracing this back to a childhood experience of harsh criticism can help you understand why you feel this way.

In 1920, John Watson and Rosalie Rayner conducted the famous "Little Albert" experiment, where they conditioned a young child to fear a white rat by pairing it with a loud, frightening noise. Over time, Albert began to fear not only the rat but also other similar objects, such as a white rabbit. This experiment showed how emotional responses can be conditioned, and how past experiences can lead to irrational fears and anxieties.

You may not realize how much you're still holding onto irrational fears and anxieties. Once you do, you'll be able to break the negative patterns they've created. For example, if you were bullied as a child and now you avoid social situations, you may start to notice this connection between the past and the present. Now you can start working on overcoming this pattern and build healthier social connections.

Understanding your emotional triggers can help you manage your reactions better. Here are some reflective questions to help you dig into your past experiences and see how they affect you today.

Identifying Your Emotional Triggers: Reflective Questions

Personal Experiences

1. **Supportive and Encouraging Parents:**
    - Did my parents or caregivers encourage me when I was growing up?
    - How did their support, or lack of it, affect my confidence?
    - Can I think of specific moments where their encouragement made me feel secure and confident?

2. **Harsh Criticism:**
    - Were my mistakes criticized more than my achievements celebrated?
    - How did constant criticism affect my self-esteem?
    - Do I now feel like I'm never good enough or fear failure because of this?
    - How do I handle challenges or setbacks today?

School Environment and Teachers

3. **Positive Reinforcement:**
    - Did any teachers help boost my self-confidence?
    - Can I remember a time when a teacher made me believe in myself?
    - How do positive memories from school influence how I learn or see myself now?

4. **Negative Experiences:**
    - Did I experience bullying or unfair treatment at school?
    - How did these negative experiences affect my ability to trust others and feel good about myself?
    - Are there any lasting emotional wounds from school that affect how I interact with people today?

Peer Interactions

5. **Supportive Friendships:**
    - Did I have friends who supported me as I grew up?
    - How did these friendships help me through the challenges of childhood?
    - What did I learn about trust and empathy from my childhood friends?

6. **Exclusion or Betrayal:**
    - Have I been excluded or betrayed by friends when I was younger?
    - How did these experiences affect my ability to trust others?
    - Do I feel anxious in social situations because of past betrayals or judgements?
    - How do these early experiences influence my current relationships and social interactions?

By asking yourself these questions, you can understand your emotional triggers and the impact of your past experiences on your present emotional responses. This self-awareness is the first step towards managing and regulating your emotions effectively.

I know this exercise might be uncomfortable and may bring up unwanted memories, but understanding these patterns helps us recognize why certain situations trigger strong emotional reactions. Knowing the origins of your emotional responses gives you the power to change. If you understand that certain behaviour is a learned response from past experiences, you can consciously work to change it.

Think of it like cleaning out a closet. When you avoid looking at the clutter, it just keeps piling up, making it harder to find what you need. But when you take the time to sort through it, you can throw away what's no longer useful, keep what's valuable, and make space for new, better things. Similarly, reflecting on past experiences allows you to declutter your mind. You can let go of what no longer serves you making room for personal growth and positive change.

I know this journey isn't easy—it may require revisiting painful memories and confronting old wounds—but the reward is a life no longer controlled by the damage of the past.

Practical Exercise

1. **Trigger Awareness Log**
- **Objective**: Identify emotional triggers and understand your reactions.
- **Instructions**:
    1. Keep a journal for a week and record any situation where you felt a strong emotional reaction (e.g., anger, frustration, sadness).
    2. Write down what happened, how you felt, and what thoughts went through your mind.
    3. Reflect on whether these emotions were justified or exaggerated by a deeper, unresolved issue.

4. At the end of the week, look for patterns in the situations that trigger your emotions.
- **Source**: Adapted from mindfulness practices and cognitive behavioural therapy (CBT) principles for emotional awareness.

2. **Name and Tame the Emotion**
   - **Objective**: Gain control over intense emotions by labelling them.
   - **Instructions**:
      1. The next time you feel triggered, pause for a moment and take a deep breath.
      2. Name the emotion you're feeling (e.g., "I feel angry," "I feel anxious").
      3. Ask yourself, "Why do I feel this way? Is this emotion based on a current reality, or is it tied to a past experience or fear?"
      4. By naming the emotion and its cause, you can tame its intensity.
   - **Source**: This exercise is inspired by the mindfulness technique "name it to tame it," based on research by Dr. Dan Siegel.

Chapter - 8

Taking Control Of Emotional Triggers

*"Triggers are the guides to healing. We can learn to notice them, explore them, and defuse them." - **Arianna Huffington**.*

Once you learn to identify what triggers you and sends you in a downward spiral, it's time for action. Here is a five-step process to learn to manage your triggers.

Step 1: Learn from the triggers: What is the trigger trying to teach you? Each triggered moment is an opportunity for growth and self-discovery. Reflect on what you've learned about yourself and how you can use that insight to improve future responses.

For example, let's say you're in a team meeting at work, and a colleague dismisses your idea without much consideration. You immediately feel a rush of anger and embarrassment, and your mind starts racing with thoughts like, "They never take me seriously," or "I'm not good enough to be here." You spend the rest of the meeting thinking about the incident, and it affects your mood for the rest of the day.

What you can learn from this trigger:

1. *Unresolved Emotions:* Triggers often reveal emotions you haven't fully processed. The strong emotional reaction of anger and embarrassment you felt suggests there's an unresolved issue you haven't dealt with yet. Perhaps you've experienced similar situations in the past where you felt dismissed or undervalued, and those emotions are resurfacing now.

2. ***Core Beliefs****:* Triggers can expose core beliefs we hold about ourselves and the world. These beliefs might be negative or limiting, such as feeling unworthy, fearing failure, or believing that the world is unsafe. The thoughts that follow your reaction ("I'm not good enough") reveal a limiting belief about your self-worth. This belief may be the result of past experiences where you felt inadequate or overlooked.

3. ***Areas for Growth****:* Triggers point to areas where we can grow emotionally. They show us where we might need to develop more resilience, self-compassion, or emotional regulation. Instead of letting the trigger control your mood for the rest of the day, you could learn to process the emotion in the moment and respond more constructively.

Step 2. Stay in the present moment: Often when we get triggered, we lose sense of the present moment, get lost in our own thoughts, and start cooking up negative stories about the thing that triggered us. To prevent yourself from doing this, observe your emotions without reacting impulsively. Use grounding techniques to stay connected to the present moment. This could be as simple as focusing on your breath. This practice is also known as mindfulness.

A study published in the journal 'Emotion' in 2010 by Keng, Smoski, and Robins explored the impact of mindfulness on emotional regulation. The researchers found that individuals who practiced mindfulness were better at managing their emotional responses to triggers. By staying present and observing their thoughts without judgment, participants were less likely to react impulsively to negative emotions.

Step 3: Set Boundaries: Triggers can highlight where our boundaries lie and whether they've been crossed. Figure out which situations or people consistently trigger negative emotions. Set boundaries to protect your emotional well-being. Don't bother about trying to impress someone or trying to keep the peace. Trying to keep the peace will only start a war within yourself. So, don't be afraid to clearly communicate your boundaries to others, explaining what you need to feel safe and respected. Be firm but respectful in enforcing these boundaries.

In the above example, the trigger indicates that you value respect and consideration in your workplace interactions. The frustration you feel might be a sign that you need to communicate your boundaries more clearly or address the issue directly with your colleagues.

Step 4: Visualize Success: Regularly visualize yourself responding to triggers in a calm way. Visualization helps train your brain to react differently in real-life situations. Think of potential scenarios where you might be triggered and mentally rehearse how you'll respond. This prepares you for real-life situations.

Step 5: Seek Support When Needed: If your triggers are deeply rooted or cause significant distress, get help from a therapist or counsellor. They can provide tools and strategies to manage your triggers effectively if you are unable to do it yourself.

One of my friends often found herself constantly irritated by her boss's feedback. Every time her boss pointed out an area for improvement, she'd feel scared and angry. When we were discussing this issue, I suggested that she apply these steps to manage her triggers. She decided to give it a try and started reflecting on her reactions. Much to her surprise, she recognized a pattern: her father had been highly critical during her childhood, and any form of feedback now triggered those old feelings of inadequacy. When she understood this, she was able to see her boss's feedback as a tool for growth rather than a personal attack. She worked on this trigger and developed healthier ways to respond. She no longer looked at feedback as criticism. Ultimately, she was free from the trigger.

If you want to experience true emotional freedom, recognizing and managing emotional triggers is the way to go.

Practical Exercises

1. Grounding Technique: 5-4-3-2-1 Method

Objective: Reduce emotional overwhelm by focusing on the present moment.

Instructions: When you feel emotionally triggered, stop and ground yourself using the 5-4-3-2-1 technique:

5: Acknowledge 5 things you can see around you.

4: Acknowledge 4 things you can touch.

3: Acknowledge 3 things you can hear.

2: Acknowledge 2 things you can smell.

1: Acknowledge 1 thing you can taste.

By grounding yourself in the present, you can prevent emotional triggers from spiralling out of control.

2. *The "What's Really Going On?" Reflection*

Objective: Discover the root of your triggers to manage them more effectively.

Instructions:

1. After being triggered, ask yourself:

"What's really bothering me here?"

"Am I reacting to this particular event, or is it tapping into something deeper, like past hurt or fear?"

2. Write down the root cause you uncover. For example, you might find that your anger is less about the specific event and more about feeling undervalued over time.

This reflection helps you get to the heart of why certain things trigger you and enables you to deal with those emotions proactively.

Source: Inspired by self-awareness exercises from emotional intelligence practices.

3. *Develop an Action Plan for Your Triggers*

Objective: Create a strategy to handle emotional triggers in the future.

Instructions:

1. Pick one emotional trigger that repeatedly bothers you (e.g., feeling criticized).

2. Write down what usually happens and how you typically react.
   - Now, create an action plan for the next time it happens:
   - How will you pause and respond?
   - What calming technique will you use (e.g., deep breathing)?
   - What will you remind yourself of (e.g., "This is temporary, I can handle this")?

3. Practice this plan when the trigger occurs again.

Source: Inspired by cognitive-behavioural techniques for behaviour modification

Chapter - 9
How Your Brain Processes Emotions

*"Neuroscience teaches us that emotions are not just feelings; they are the brain's responses to the challenges of life." -**Unknown.***

Think of your brain as the control room in a high-tech command centre from a sci-fi movie. There are departments for carrying out different tasks. One of the departments is responsible for managing your emotions. The leader of this department is a part of your brain called the amygdala. You can think of the amygdala as the chief security officer of your brain. Its job is to scan the environment for any signs of danger. When it spots something that might be a threat, it immediately sounds the alarm, just like a security system does when it detects an intruder.

Let's say you're walking in a park, and suddenly, you see a snake crossing your path. Your amygdala instantly recognizes the danger and hits the panic button. Within a split second, your body reacts before you even have time to think. You might start shaking, your heart races, your breathing quickens, and your palms get sweaty. These reactions prepare you to either fight the snake or run away as fast as you can. This happens so quickly that your brain barely has time to think, "Whoa, that's a snake!" before your body is already reacting.

This is known as the amygdala hijack. The amygdala, which is a part of your brain, is responsible for sensing danger and sending out a distress signal. When the amygdala detects a threat, it triggers the release of stress hormones like adrenaline and cortisol, preparing your body to either fight, flee, or even freeze. This response happens incredibly fast, ensuring that you're protected in an instant.

The amygdala doesn't just respond to physical threats; it also reacts to emotional ones, like criticism or rejection. Over time, these reactions can create negative thinking patterns and beliefs. In simpler terms, past negative experiences can program your amygdala to overreact in certain situations, even when there's no real danger.

Example 1: If you were often told you weren't good enough as a child and other kids were better than you, your amygdala might have started to associate certain situations, like public speaking or taking on new challenges, with that same feeling of inadequacy. So, if you were put in a situation where you have to speak before an audience, it would trigger a fear response, making you believe, "I can't do this," even when you're perfectly capable if you really tried. So, you can see how a long-term thought like "I am not good enough" affects your short-term reactions.

Example 2: Sana's ex-boyfriend frequently criticized her and made her feel unworthy. She is now in a healthy relationship but her experience with her ex has left a deep emotional scar. Her amygdala has learned to associate criticism with feelings of hurt and rejection. Her new boyfriend is kind and funny. But if he makes a light-hearted comment about something minor, she reacts immediately with anger, defensiveness, or anxiety. She fears he might leave her if he finds a single fault in her.

Even though her new boyfriend's intentions are not to hurt her, Sana's amygdala remembers the past pain. It triggers an emotional response similar to what she felt in her previous relationship. Her brain is trying to protect her based on her past experience. It doesn't recognize that this new partner is different, and the context has changed. Instead, it simply reacts to what it believes is a similar trigger.

The Prefrontal Cortex

Let's move on to another department in your brain: The prefrontal cortex. It's located at the front of your brain and is responsible for important functions like decision-making, self-control, and managing your emotions. As we just discussed, the amygdala is like your brain's alarm system. Its job is to detect threats and protect you. When you face a stressful situation, your amygdala can hijack your brain's responses, causing you to react out of emotion before your prefrontal cortex (the wise one) has a chance to come up with a more thoughtful decision.

This is because the prefrontal cortex processes information more slowly. It evaluates the situation, considers various options, and decides on the best course of action. In moments of immediate threat, this is time-consuming. However, we can all agree that in everyday situations where the threat isn't immediate, we should rely on the prefrontal cortex. If only Sana (from example 2 above) knew how to use her prefrontal cortex and tell it to take charge, she would be able to react in a healthier way and form a great relationship with her current partner.

You might wonder, why isn't it easy for us? When you're stressed or tired, the prefrontal cortex (the part of your brain that helps you think clearly) doesn't work as well as it should. So, your brain often lets the amygdala take control. The amygdala is quicker to react, but it can sometimes make you respond in a way that isn't logical. Controlling your reactions and thinking calmly isn't always easy, but there are ways to strengthen the connection between the amygdala and the prefrontal cortex of your brain. This can help you stay calm and think more clearly.

Let's see how you can use your prefrontal cortex to your advantage.

1. *Practice Meditation*

Meditation strengthens the prefrontal cortex, which enhances your ability to stay calm and think clearly. Studies have shown that regions of the prefrontal cortex are larger in meditators than in non-meditators. So, if you meditate, you will boost your ability to manage your emotions, stay focused and make good decisions.

Additionally, in meditators, the amygdala shrank in size, and they reported feeling less stressed. We know how our amygdala has a hold on our emotional responses. If it shrinks, this hold can be reduced, and you can experience emotional freedom. With regular meditation, you become less reactive to what happens to you or in your surroundings and can stay calm in any situation. That's why one of the scientific benefits of meditation is a greater ability to regulate our emotions.

Spend a few minutes each day practicing meditation. Apps like Headspace or Calm can guide you through the process. You can also follow guided meditations on YouTube.

2. Create a Decision-Making Process

Structured decision-making engages the prefrontal cortex, helping you make choices based on logic rather than raw emotion. List pros and cons or write down your feelings and potential actions before reacting. Look at the situation from the perspective of an outsider.

3. Engage in Rational Thinking

When you feel overwhelmed, pause and ask yourself logical questions. For example, "What evidence do I have that this situation is as bad as it seems?" or "What are the long-term benefits of handling this calmly?" "Will this improve my relationship with the person before me or deteriorate it? This helps the prefrontal cortex override impulsive emotional reactions and support more thoughtful decision-making. One way to apply this is the following technique.

The "Pause and Pivot" Technique

My good friend Rick Cormier, a psychotherapist, introduced me to this technique. The Pause and Pivot technique works by first giving you a moment to pause and acknowledge your emotions. It gives you a chance to use your rational brain. Creating that small space between feeling and reacting can make a huge difference in handling emotions.

How to Practice the "Pause and Pivot" Technique:

1. **Pause:** When you feel a strong emotion rising, immediately take a moment to pause. This pause doesn't have to be long—just a few seconds can make a difference. During this pause, take a deep breath. It helps activate the parasympathetic nervous system, which calms your body and reduces the intensity of the emotion.

2. **Name Your Emotion:** Identify the emotion you are feeling. It could be anger, sadness, anxiety, or frustration. Naming your emotions helps you understand and process them.

3. **Pivot:** After naming your emotion, consciously choose to shift your focus. Ask yourself:
    1. What is one small action I can take right now to feel better?
    2. How can I view this situation differently?
    3. What positive outcome can I aim for in this moment?

4. **Take Action:** Take a small, positive action. This could be anything from going for a walk, listening to music, working out, or talking to a friend. The pivot allows you to turn a negative emotion into positive action, shifting your behaviour patterns.

Example: Applying the Pause-Pivot-Action Cycle

If your partner points out a mistake you made or a behaviour that bothers them, your immediate emotional response might be anger and frustration. You might get defensive and respond with anger or remind them of the mistakes they might have made long ago. However, if you take a moment to pause, you can respond more thoughtfully. Here's how that might look like using the Pause-Pivot-Action Cycle:

1. **Pause**: When they start talking about your mistakes, take a deep breath to calm your initial emotional response. This moment between emotion (anger) and action (starting a fight) is golden. Your job is to prolong this time gap.

2. **Name it**: Recognize and name the emotion you're experiencing. You might name it as anger. Identify the source of the emotion. It could be the fear of appearing less than perfect in your partner's eyes or losing their affection. It could also be the feeling of being misunderstood by your partner that is making you feel angry.

3. **Pivot**: Shift your focus by asking a few questions to reframe the situation positively. For example, ask yourself,

    "Is the criticism entirely unfair, or is there something I can learn from this?"

"How can I turn this into an opportunity to make the relationship better?"

"Will my response bring me closer to my partner or push us further apart?"

4. **Action**: Take constructive action. Instead of reacting impulsively, decide to acknowledge the mistake, apologize if you need to, and outline a plan to fix the issue. Or if you believe that the criticism wasn't fair, you could decide to discuss it later. You're not avoiding the issue. You're only giving your emotions a chance to cool down so that you can respond when you can think clearly.

This is how you can use your prefrontal cortex to handle emotional situations thoughtfully and effectively. With practice, you will find that this approach not only helps you manage your emotions but also prevents misunderstandings and strengthens your relationship.

The Hand Model

The hand model of the brain, created by Dr. Daniel Siegel is another very simple tool that you can use to handle your emotions. It can also help you understand and remember the concept of amygdala. This model helps visualize the brain's structure and functions, especially regarding emotional reactions.

1. **Make a Fist**: Start by making a fist with your thumb tucked inside your fingers. Imagine that this is your brain.

    - **The Wrist and Palm**: Your wrist and the base of your palm represent the brainstem, responsible for basic survival functions.
    - **The Thumb**: Your thumb, tucked inside, represents the amygdala which handles your emotions.
    - **The Fingers**: Your fingers, represent the prefrontal cortex, responsible for clear thinking, decision-making, and self-control. When your fingers are folded over the thumb, it shows that your prefrontal cortex is taking charge of your emotions.

2. **Amygdala Hijacking**: When you experience a highly stressful or threatening situation, the amygdala becomes active, causing an immediate emotional reaction. To imagine this, open your fingers, exposing the thumb.

   - **Exposed Thumb**: When the amygdala is triggered, it can override the prefrontal cortex, leading to impulsive reactions without rational thought. This is like "flipping your lid," where the emotional brain takes over.

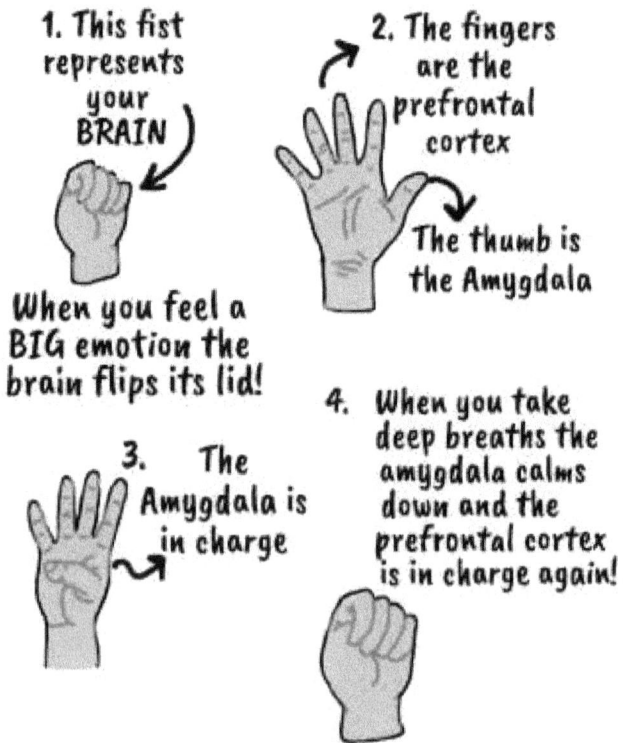

Using the Hand Model to Manage Amygdala Hijacking

Here's how you can use the hand model to manage your emotions:

1. **Recognize the Signs**: When you feel an intense emotional reaction building up, look at your thumb and recognize that your amygdala might be taking control.

2. **Pause and Breathe**: Take a moment to breathe deeply and calm yourself. This can help re-engage the prefrontal cortex, bringing rational thinking back into the picture. Flip your fingers to cover the thumb and visualize that you are gaining control over your amygdala.

3. **Reassess the Situation**: The fingers folded over the thumb is a sign to let your prefrontal cortex take control. You know how to do that: by asking questions. Ask yourself if your immediate reaction is based on the current reality or if it's an emotional response driven by the amygdala. This pause can help you choose a more measured and thoughtful response.

Your brain can be your friend or your enemy depending on how you use it. As Viktor Frankl once said, "Between stimulus and response, there is a space. In that space is our power to choose our response. In our response lies our growth and our freedom." This is a timeless principle and has been repeated by wise thinkers from the ancient era. It is very similar to the modern understanding of how our brain and thoughts shape our emotional experiences. When you learn to use the power of your brain, you can transform your reactions and ultimately, your life.

Chapter - 10

Reconnect With Happiness Using Your Hippocampus

"To live in the past is to die in the present, but to learn from the past is to live fully." - **Unknown.**

Like a librarian, the hippocampus is a part of your brain that stores and recollects memories. It helps you understand your emotions by connecting them to past experiences. For example, if you feel happy when you smell a certain perfume, it's because the hippocampus linked that scent to a happy memory from your past. You must have experienced this: you're driving and hear a song on the radio that you used to listen to during a happy period in your life, like a fun summer vacation or joyful times with friends. Suddenly, you're flooded with memories of sunny days, laughter, and carefree moments. This is your hippocampus at work. It brings back the memories associated with that song, feelings of happiness, and nostalgia. You might have noticed that your parents prefer to listen to songs from the old era. It's because their brain has made a connection with those songs. The hippocampus helps bridge the past with the present.

You can use this part of the brain to instantly shift your emotions when you're feeling low. If you think of happy memories or play a song that made you feel happy in the past, you will notice your emotional state quickly shift from negative to positive. This memory retrieval function helps overcome tough situations too. For example, if you are going through a breakup, ask yourself, what helped you recover from previous breakups? Maybe, focusing on self-care helped you recover. Remind yourself to do that now. Think about specific self-care activities that worked for you, like taking long walks, reading a favourite book, or spending time with friends who uplift you. As you try to remember these things, you will also remember that even though you felt so low during that time, you could get yourself out of it and be happy again. In a way, revisiting these experiences and remembering what worked in the past can give you strength and guidance for your current situation.

So, to make the most of your hippocampus, here's what you can do:

1. *Reflect on past experiences*

Journaling is a powerful tool for this. Write about how you got over past challenges and what strategies worked best. This activates the hippocampus, helping you seek wisdom from past experiences to manage current feelings and decisions more effectively.

2. *Create new positive associations*

Instead of avoiding places or activities that remind you of painful experiences, you can reshape your emotional connection to them by creating new, positive memories in those same spaces. For example, if you and your ex used to visit a particular café, don't avoid it. Go there with friends to celebrate birthdays, and career milestones, or simply to enjoy your time. Over time, these joyful experiences will begin to overwrite the old, negative associations.

3. *Focus on Happy Memories*

Just say, Expecto Patronum! In the Harry Potter series, Harry learns a difficult spell called the Patronus charm. It's used to repel Dementors, which are dangerous creatures that feed on negative emotions (for those unfamiliar with the series). To cast the spell, a wizard has to think of the happiest moments in their life, which is not easy when you're facing something terrifying. That's why the spell is for advanced wizards. This concept is so relevant to real life.

Thinking of happy memories when you are feeling down could be challenging, but you can bring up happy memories as a defence mechanism against the negative thoughts and feelings which are the dementors of your life. So, try this: When you're feeling down, take a moment to consciously think about joyful moments from your past. To make it easier, you can look through old photos from a family vacation or remember that fun night out with friends. You can rewatch movies that make you feel good. Maybe you have a video of your trip where everyone was dancing and having a great time—watching it again can bring back those positive feelings.

Practical Exercises: Reconnect with Happiness Using Your Hippocampus

Exercise 1: Memory Journaling

Instructions: Take a moment to reflect on past challenges you've overcome. Write about how you managed those situations and what strategies worked best for you.

1. **Describe a Challenge You've Overcome:**
   - What was the situation?
   - How did it make you feel at the time?

2. **Reflect on the Strategies You Used:**
   - What actions did you take to overcome the challenge?
   - Which strategies were most effective?
   - How did these strategies help you emotionally?

3. **Lesson Learned:**
   - What did you learn from this experience?
   - How can these lessons help you with current challenges?

Exercise 2: Creating New Positive Associations

Instructions: Find an activity that makes you feel good and plan how you can engage in this activity more often. If possible, create new positive memories in places or situations that were once associated with negative emotions.

1. **Choose an Activity You Enjoy:**
   - What is an activity that brings you joy (e.g., painting, hiking, cooking)?
   - How often do you currently engage in this activity?

2. **Plan to Engage in This Activity:**

- How can you make more time for this activity in your life?
- Can you invite friends or loved ones to join you to create new, positive memories?

3. **REFRAME a Negative Memory:**
   - Is there a place or situation that you associate with negative emotions?
   - How can you create a new, positive experience in that context (e.g., visiting a café with friends that you used to go to with an ex)?

Exercise 3: Focusing on Happy Memories

Instructions: Practice recalling happy memories, especially during moments of stress or sadness. Use this exercise to shift your emotional state from negative to positive.

1. **Think of a Happy Memory:**
   - Think of a specific memory that brings you joy (e.g., a family vacation, or a special celebration).
   - Describe this memory in detail.

2. **Visualize and Reflect:**
   - Close your eyes and visualize the memory. What do you see, hear, smell, or feel?
   - How does this memory make you feel emotionally?

3. **Use Happy Memories as a Tool:**
   - Next time you feel down, consciously recall this memory.
   - How did recalling the memory affect your mood?
   - How can you use this technique regularly to boost your emotional well-being?

Exercise 4: Visualization and Future Planning

Instructions: Visualize a positive outcome in a current situation where you feel stuck or challenged.

1. **Identify a Current Challenge:**
   - What challenge are you currently facing?
   - How does it make you feel?

2. **Visualize a Positive Outcome:**
   - Imagine a future where this challenge is resolved. What does that look like?
   - How do you feel in this positive future?

3. **Plan Your Next Steps:**
   - What actions can you take now to move towards that positive outcome?

Exercise 5: Reflecting on Past Relationships

Instructions: Use your memory of past relationships to guide your current situation. This exercise helps you apply what you've learned from past experiences to improve your emotional well-being.

1. **Recall a Past Relationship:**
   - Think of a past relationship that ended. How did it affect you emotionally?

2. **Identify What Helped You Heal:**
   - What activities, people, or thoughts helped you heal from that breakup?
   - How did you feel after engaging in those activities or spending time with those people?

3. **Apply to Current Situation:**
   - Are you facing a similar situation now?
   - How can you apply the same healing strategies to your current emotional challenges?

Chapter - 11
The Power of Neuroplasticity In Emotional Healing

*"The ability of the brain to change its physical structure and function in response to experience is known as neuroplasticity. This is the foundation of emotional healing." - **Norman Doidge.***

If you have ever watched a motivational video, the speaker always says, "You have no limits, you can achieve anything", right? I used to think it was just something that felt good to listen to, but not practical for real life. After a certain age, we are set in our ways. We believe that we can no longer learn new skills, make new friends, or discover new talents. Scientists used to think that too! Up until the 1970s, neuroscientists believed that the brain's structure and function were essentially fixed throughout adulthood. But then, they discovered something amazing: Neuroplasticity.

So, what is Neuroplasticity? It's the brain's ability to change and adapt throughout life. When we learn something new, our brain forms new neural connections and strengthens existing ones. This is backed by numerous scientific studies, such as one published in the Journal of Neuroscience, which found that learning a new skill can change the brain's structure. Your brain can rewire itself to improve and adapt as required.

Neuroplasticity also helps the brain recover from brain injury. Such is the power of your amazing brain. Studies on monkeys and humans show that if a part of the brain is damaged, neighbouring brain areas can carry out functions of the damaged regions.

> *If you can literally heal your brain like this, why do you think you cannot recover from heartbreak or anything else that has caused you emotional suffering? It's ironic how we underestimate our own abilities to overcome challenges when our brain is so capable.*

The amazing thing about neuroplasticity is that it means you're not stuck with the brain you were born with. You can literally change the structure and function of your brain by changing the way you think, feel, and act. You can create an entirely new version of yourself and your life. So, you must understand and learn to harness this power to rewire your brain.

The Science Behind Neuroplasticity

To challenge your negative thoughts and limiting beliefs that have formed over many years, you need to put effort into creating new neural pathways. How? Start by noticing the negative thoughts and questioning if they are really true. See if they are based on facts or just a result of past experiences. That's what we learned to do in Step 1, right? In this step, we will understand how to go beyond that by understanding our brain on a deeper level.

Think of your brain as a big forest with many twisting and interconnecting paths. What will happen if someone walks a particular path to travel through the forest every day? It will become clearer, more defined, and easier to take. That's what happens in your brain. Each time you have a thought, you create and strengthen these paths. When you repeat a particular thought or behaviour, the path becomes clearer and more defined just like a well-trodden trail in the forest.

> *If you keep thinking negative thoughts, like "I'm not good enough," the neurons of your brain create a strong path, making it easier for that thought to come up again in the future.*

Research has shown that if you have been feeling stressed for a long time, it can mess with your brain's ability to form new neural connections which can contribute to the development of depression. Also, chronic stress means you're repeating negative thoughts. Because of neuroplasticity, the brain strengthens the neural pathways that are associated with stress-creating thoughts, and it becomes easier to get stressed again.

Neuroplasticity can work for you or against you depending on your level of awareness of your emotions and your ability to redirect your thoughts.

We want to educate ourselves to use this incredible power of our brain for growth in a positive direction. That's the essence of true healing: *change and growth in a positive direction.* So, let's see how neuroplasticity can help you overcome emotional challenges and heal. Now that you have understood the science behind neuroplasticity, you can see that neuroplasticity is the perfect tool for change and growth in a positive direction regardless of past experiences or current emotional challenges. There are many ways to harness neuroplasticity. But the following three are the most practical for daily life.

Practical Applications of Neuroplasticity for emotional healing and rewiring negative thought patterns

1. Meditation:

Meditation and Rewiring Negative Thought Patterns:

The popular belief about meditation is that it's just a way to relax and calm down. In addition to its calming effects, meditation has been shown to help rewire the brain and reduce negative thought patterns. We discussed how the prefrontal cortex helps us think clearly and make decisions with self-control. But it's not easy to be aware of our thoughts, especially when we are under the influence of our emotions. When you meditate regularly, you increase the activity in the prefrontal cortex. This helps you recognize negative thought patterns as they arise and consciously choose to redirect them. Over time, this practice strengthens the neural pathways associated with positive thinking, which can help break the cycle of automatic negative thoughts.

Mindfulness Meditation and Emotional Healing:

Mindfulness meditation is about focusing on the present moment and observing your emotions without being attached to them. It's particularly helpful for healing emotional wounds because it encourages you to accept your thoughts and feelings without judgement.

In *The Power of Now*, Eckhart Tolle emphasizes that living in the present moment is key to freeing yourself from mental patterns that cause emotional pain. Much of our suffering comes from being trapped in thoughts about the past or future. Mindfulness allows you to stay in the "now," where true peace and healing occurs. In his book, he also talks about the concept of the *pain-body*, which is the accumulation of past emotional pain that can be triggered in the present. Mindfulness meditation helps you become aware of this pain-body without letting it control you, creating space for emotional release and healing.

Additionally, neuroscientific research shows that mindfulness meditation increases Gray matter density in the brain, particularly in areas related to memory, learning, and emotional processing. This supports your ability to manage emotions more effectively, creating both short-term relief and long-term emotional resilience.

Meditation and Stress Reduction:

When you're stressed, your brain releases cortisol. This hormone can damage neural connections over time if it's continuously present. Meditation has been shown to lower cortisol levels and protect your brain from the harmful effects of chronic stress. It also enhances the brain's ability to recover from stressful situations more quickly, which can improve emotional resilience.

Building Positive Habits through Meditation:

Because of neuroplasticity, the more you engage in meditation, the stronger the neural pathways associated with positive thoughts become. With consistent practice, these positive habits become automatic responses. This means you'll not only feel more relaxed during meditation but also experience a more peaceful mindset throughout the day, even in stressful situations.

If you have never meditated in your life before, here are simple steps to start meditating:

Find a Quiet Space:

Choose a calm, quiet spot where you won't be disturbed. Sit comfortably, either on a chair or on the floor.

Focus on Your Breath:

Close your eyes and take a few deep breaths. Then, settle into a natural breathing rhythm. Pay attention to the sensation of each breath as it enters and leaves your nostrils or the rise and fall of your chest. Count 1 on inhale and 2 on exhale until you reach the count of 10. Start with 1 again after 10.

Observe Your Thoughts:

As you meditate, thoughts will inevitably pop up. Instead of fighting them, simply observe them. Acknowledge the thought, label it as "thinking," and gently guide your focus back to your breath.

Stay Present: The goal is to remain in the present moment. If your mind wanders, which it will, gently bring it back to your breath. Start with just a few minutes a day and gradually increase the duration as you become more comfortable.

2. *Physical Exercise*

Exercise plays a powerful role in improving emotional well-being. In people with depression, the hippocampus, which is the area that regulates your emotions, is often reduced in size. This affects the brain's ability to adapt and form new connections. But exercise has the opposite effect. It helps maintain and increase the size of the hippocampus which leads to better mood regulation and a decrease in depressive symptoms.

Additionally, exercise stimulates the release of a protein called brain-derived neurotrophic factor (BDNF), which helps the brain form new neurons and connections. This supports neuroplasticity which is essential for overcoming negative thought patterns.

Regular physical activity promotes the release of neurotransmitters like serotonin and dopamine, also known as the "feel-good hormones," which help you stay in a good mood. Recent studies have shown that exercise is just as effective as psychotherapy and antidepressants in the management of mild to moderate depression. Given the side effects of antidepressants and the cost of therapy, exercise is a great option for people wanting to improve their mental health. Many therapists suggest exercise as a first step or add-on treatment for mental health issues like depression, anxiety, and stress.

So, aim to get at least 30 minutes of exercise a day—not just for your physical health, but for your emotional and mental well-being too.

3. *Learning New Skills*

When you start learning something new, your brain forms and strengthens the neural connections required for learning it. That's why even without a natural talent, you can learn anything you want to learn.

There was a time when I constantly felt overwhelmed by self-doubt. Whenever I faced a challenge, like public speaking or stepping out of my comfort zone, I would automatically think, "I can't do this" or "I'm an introvert; I can never speak confidently." These thoughts felt like a reflex. But when I learned about neuroplasticity—the brain's ability to rewire itself based on our thoughts and experiences—I realized I couldn't keep blaming my personality or making excuses for my limitations. I could no longer say, "I'm shy because that's just who I am." I understood that if my brain could change, I could break free from these limitations.

I decided to test neuroplasticity for myself. Every time a negative thought about public speaking came up, I challenged it. I'd ask myself, "Is this thought helping me?" If the answer was no, I replaced it with something more powerful, like, "I can do this because my brain can change." Along with challenging my thoughts, I also started taking online courses on public speaking, reading books on the subject, and even started a YouTube channel to practice speaking. My first videos were embarrassing, but that's the price of progress in anything.

Over time, I noticed a shift. The negative thoughts became less frequent, and the positive ones started to feel more natural. It wasn't an overnight change—there were still days where I doubted myself. But I kept practicing speaking by uploading videos on YouTube.

One day, I received an opportunity to speak at Josh Talks, India's premier speaking platform with over 4 million followers. I was excited but had only half a day to prepare my talk. Yet, I felt ready. Because I had consistently shown myself that I could speak.

On the day of the talk, in a theatre with a live audience, I spoke for 20 minutes straight. Even now, I'm amazed at how I did it. That experience strengthened my belief in the power of neuroplasticity. After that, I was invited to speak at different colleges on various topics. It was surprising that people enjoyed my talks. It was the opposite of what I had believed all my life. I had literally rewired my brain to overcome a deep-seated fear. It taught me that you can learn and excel at anything, no matter where you start or how much talent you think you have.

Imagine how exciting life could be if you opened your mind to all possibilities and learned new skills. It would add richness to your life story. It might even change the direction of your career. Now I use this power to learn anything I desire, like singing, dancing, writing, and other fun things because I see nothing holding me back anymore.

So, if you're facing a challenge in your life, know that you can rewire your brain to think positively, develop emotional strength, heal from past traumas, and transform yourself into the person you want to be. No matter what you've been through or where you are right now, everything can be changed. Your brain is designed that way!

Step - 3
REFRAME
Change The Way You Think

In this step, we'll discuss how your thoughts shape your emotions and actions and learn to reframe them using the three most effective practices. These practices will rewire you to think more positively.

1. Affirmations
2. Gratitude
3. Daily emotional detox

We will discuss the science behind these practices and how you can make these practices as easy and automatic as brushing your teeth every day.

Chapter - 12

How Your Thoughts Shape Your Emotions And Actions

*The way we think influences the way we feel, and the way we feel influences the way we act. Change one, and you change all." - **Unknown**.*

Our current reality is shaped by our past thoughts and actions, just like a movie you're watching was filmed well before you ever saw it. What you see on screen isn't happening in the present moment—it was created long ago. The "movie" of your life that you're experiencing now was shaped by your previous thoughts and actions. If you start changing your thoughts and behaviours today, you'll create a future that's brighter and more positive—your next "movie" will be one you're excited to watch.

Imagine your thoughts, emotions, and behaviours as three corners of a triangle. They constantly interact with each other, creating a dynamic loop that affects your mental and emotional well-being. This concept, known as the cognitive-behavioural model, can be incredibly empowering once you understand it.

Thoughts

Your thoughts are the mental chatter that runs through your mind, but they are incredibly powerful because they shape how you feel and behave even if they are not true sometimes.

For example, consider a common thought, "I'm not good enough." This negative thought can trigger feelings of sadness or anxiety. Thoughts can create beliefs if they are repeated. If you continually think that you are not good enough, it will turn into a deep belief, influencing your self-esteem and confidence. Because of this belief, you will avoid doing things that are out of your comfort zone. On the other hand, a positive thought like, "I am capable of handling this," can make you feel confident and calm and encourage you to take on challenges and believe in your abilities. So, you need to learn to cultivate more positive thoughts because they directly influence your actions/behaviour.

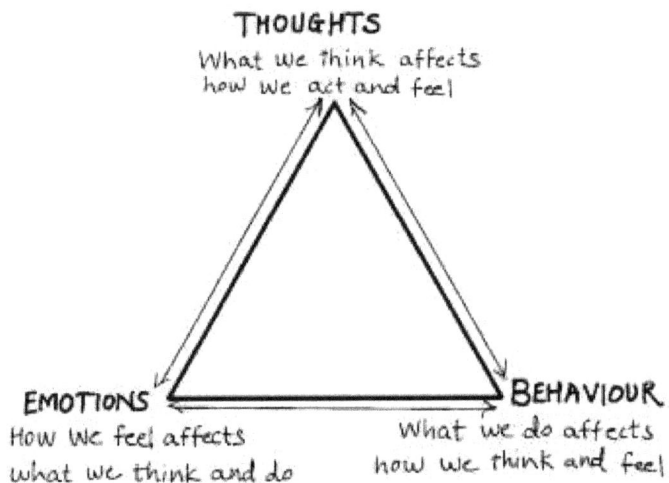

Emotions

Emotions are the internal responses to your thoughts. They are the feelings you experience, such as happiness, sadness, anger, or fear. Emotions are often temporary, lasting only a few seconds, or they can linger, influencing your mood for hours or even days. When you think negatively, you'll feel negative emotions. The longer you think negatively, the longer you will feel negative emotions.

For example, dwelling on a mistake can lead to feelings of guilt or shame. These emotions can be intense and long-lasting if the negative thought is persistent. On the flip side, thinking positively about a situation can lead to feelings of joy and satisfaction. For instance, reflecting on a personal achievement can make you feel proud and content.

Behaviours

Behaviours are the actions you take in response to your thoughts and emotions. These actions can further reinforce your thoughts and emotions, creating a feedback loop. For example, if you believe you're not good enough (thought), you might avoid challenging tasks (behaviour). This avoidance behaviour then reinforces your belief that you can't handle challenges, perpetuating the cycle.

Conversely, if you have the thought, "I am capable," you might take on a new project at work (behaviour), which can lead to feelings of accomplishment and reinforce the positive belief. Behaviours are powerful because they can either break or strengthen the cycle of negative thoughts and emotions.

When you understand the triangle of thoughts, emotions, and behaviours, you can identify negative cycles in your life. Recognizing that a negative thought is leading to harmful emotions and behaviours allows you to intervene and change your thought patterns.

The Feedback Loop

The interaction between your thoughts, emotions, and behaviours creates a feedback loop. This means that each part influences and is influenced by the others. By changing a negative pattern in one area, you can positively affect the other areas.

Example:

Negative Cycle:

1. **Negative Thought:** "No one likes me; I'm always left out."

2. **Negative Emotion:** You feel lonely and insecure.

3. **Negative Behaviour:** You withdraw from social situations and avoid reaching out to others.
   - This withdrawal makes you believe even more strongly that people don't want to be around you, which makes you feel lonelier and makes you avoid people.

Positive Cycle:

1. **Positive Thought:** "I can connect with others and build friendships."

2. **Positive Emotion:** You feel hopeful and open to new experiences.

3. **Positive Behaviour:** You start conversations and join social activities.

   - When you take the lead in starting a conversation with others, it creates opportunities for connection. This confirms your positive thoughts, boosts your confidence, and encourages you to keep building relationships.

Understanding this triad gives you the power to make intentional changes. Here's how you can use it for better emotional health:

Area	Strategy	Details
Monitor Your Thoughts	Self-Awareness	Pay attention to your self-talk. Notice negative or unhelpful thoughts and question their truth.
	Reframe	Replace negative thoughts with more positive ones. For example, instead of thinking, "I can't do this," think, "I can learn and improve."
Manage Your Emotions	Mindfulness	Practice mindfulness to stay present and aware of your emotions without judging them. This helps you understand your emotional responses better.
	Emotional Regulation	Use techniques like deep breathing, meditation, or journaling to manage intense emotions. These methods can help you stay calm and centred.
Modify Your Behaviours	Action Steps	Take small, positive actions that take you closer to your goals.
	Consistency	Make these positive behaviours a regular part of your routine to boost positive thoughts and emotions.

Personal Example:

As I am writing this book, I am feeling anxious about the outcome of this book. So, here is how I will use this thought-emotion-behaviour triad:

Area	Strategy	Personal Application
Monitor My Thoughts	Self-Awareness	"I'm not sure if my writing is good enough."
	Reframe	"I have valuable insights and experiences to share, and I can always improve my writing skills as I write more."
Manage My Emotions	Mindfulness	Focusing on writing the next sentence instead of worrying about the whole book. Staying in the present moment to reduce anxiety.
	Emotional Regulation	Deep breathing exercises before writing sessions to calm the mind. Journaling about my anxieties to understand them better.
Modify My Behaviours	Action Steps	Set a goal to write for just 20 minutes each day. Break the task into smaller sections, such as focusing on one chapter or even one paragraph at a time.
	Consistency	Make writing a consistent part of my daily routine. Celebrate small victories, like completing a section or receiving positive feedback from someone.

This is how I'll create a positive feedback loop that will control my anxiety and help me achieve my goal of getting this book published. If you are reading it, it means this strategy has worked for me.

The key takeaway here is simple: Positive thoughts lead to positive emotions, which then encourage healthier behaviours and a more balanced emotional state. Basically, your thoughts are the foundation of this cycle.

To help you pinpoint and manage negative thoughts effectively, we'll explore some more practical tools and strategies.

Practical exercises:

1. *Socratic Questioning:*

Socratic questioning is named after the ancient Greek philosopher Socrates, who lived around 470-399 BC. He was famous for his method of teaching through asking questions. Instead of giving direct answers, Socrates used to ask questions to help people dig deeper and think more clearly. Socratic questioning is like having a conversation with yourself to figure out what's really going on in your head.

When your mind starts bubbling with negative thoughts, try asking yourself these questions to challenge them and find a more balanced perspective.

1. **"What proof do I have for this thought?"**

Think of this as personal detective work. Are you sure that the thought you are thinking is based on facts, or is it just your mind's way of overreacting?

Example:

- **Negative Thought:** "I'm going to fail this presentation."
- **Proof:** Have I failed every presentation I've ever given? No, I've done well before and received positive feedback.
- **Balanced Thought:** "I've prepared well for this presentation, and I've done well in the past. There's no solid proof that I will fail. Even if I make a mistake, I'll learn something from it which will make me a better presenter in the end."

2. **"Is there another way to look at this?"**

Sometimes, your first thought isn't the only option. Try to find a different perspective because there is always more than one way of thinking about something.

Example:

- **Negative Thought:** "My friend didn't reply to my message; they must be mad at me."
- **Alternative View:** "Maybe they're busy with work or dealing with something personal. I'll give them some time and check in later."

3. **"What would I say to a friend who had this thought?"**

Imagine your friend is having the negative thought you're having. What advice would you give them? Now, be that friend to yourself and offer some kind and rational advice.

Example:

- **Negative Thought:** "My relationship ended; I'll never find love again."
- **Advice to a Friend:** "A breakup doesn't mean you're unlovable. It's a chance to learn about yourself and what you need in a relationship."
- **Changed Thought:** "This breakup is painful, but it doesn't mean I'll never find love. It's an opportunity to grow and find someone who's a better match for me."

Do you see how Socratic questioning helps you step back from your initial negative reaction and consider other possibilities? By practicing these questions regularly, you can develop a habit of thinking more rationally and kindly towards yourself. Asking these questions means you're not accepting every negative thought as your identity.

Many therapists use this technique in therapy to help people rethink their negative thoughts. Teachers use it to make students think more deeply. And you can use it to give your brain a mental workout and find a more balanced and happier outlook on life.

2. *Emotional self-reflection with the "5 Whys" technique*

Sakichi Toyoda, the founder of Toyota Industries, originally developed the "5 Whys" technique to identify the root causes of issues in their manufacturing process and enhance quality control. Because it was so effective, various industries have adopted the technique over time.

Interestingly, we can also use the "5 Whys" technique for emotional self-reflection. It can help you dig deeper into your emotions and understand the underlying reasons behind your feelings. When you are unable to find the reason behind a strong emotion like frustration or anxiety, this technique becomes a powerful tool. By asking "why" repeatedly, you can uncover the root cause of your emotions. It's like playing detective with your own feelings.

Let's say you're feeling anxious about an upcoming social event that you must attend. Instead of just sitting with that anxiety, try asking yourself "why" repeatedly—five times is usually the sweet spot. Here's how it might look in practice:

1. **Why are you feeling anxious?**
   I'm worried about attending the event alone.

2. **Why are you worried about attending the event alone?**
   I'm afraid I won't know anyone there.

3. **Why are you afraid of not knowing anyone?**
   I'm worried that I'll feel awkward or out of place.

4. **Why do you think you'll feel awkward or out of place?**
   I've had experiences in the past where I felt left out in social situations.

5. **Why do those past experiences still affect you now?**
   I haven't fully addressed or healed from those past feelings of being left out, so they still influence how I approach new social situations.

By peeling back layers like this, you can uncover a deeper understanding of your anxiety. Instead of just being nervous about attending an event alone, you realize it's tied to unresolved feelings from the past. Now you can work on the real issue using techniques mentioned in the upcoming chapters.

Chapter - 13

Changing The Narrative With Affirmations

"It's the repetition of affirmations that leads to belief. And once that belief becomes a deep conviction, things begin to happen."
- Muhammad Ali

A wise elder was teaching his grandson an important lesson about life. He said, "Within me, there is a battle going on. A fierce battle between two forces."

He went on to explain, "One force represents all the negative qualities—anger, jealousy, sorrow, regret, greed, arrogance, self-pity, guilt, resentment, and ego."

The elder paused and then said, "The other force represents everything positive—joy, peace, love, hope, humility, kindness, compassion, empathy, and truth. This same battle is happening inside you, and inside every person, every day."

The grandson thought for a while and asked, "But which force will win?"

The elder smiled gently and replied, "The one you choose to nurture."

All of us have to face the internal battle between our negative and positive thoughts and emotions. But we have the power to influence the outcome of this struggle by choosing which "wolf" to feed. Positive people consciously choose to focus on positive emotions and constructive thoughts that nurture the "good wolf" within them.

It's natural to feel all kinds of emotions but cultivating more of the positive ones can boost our happiness and well-being. Positive emotions not only make us feel good, but they also have amazing benefits. Maintaining a positive outlook helps us bounce back from setbacks and stay motivated through challenging times.

> *Positive emotions reduce stress and anxiety, promote better mental health, and make people want to be around us. You must have experienced that spending time with a positive person makes you feel cheerful too. They emit a certain kind of energy that lifts everyone who comes into contact with them. What if you could be that person for other people?*

You can learn to be a positive person using a few simple techniques discussed in this step. It's not important how many techniques you know. The internet is flooded with information about all these tools that can make you more positive. However, deeply understanding and practicing only a few of the most effective ones is the smart and sustainable thing to do.

You're affirming all the time.

We think thousands of thoughts every day, but most of us don't realize how they affect us. If you spend a day noticing every thought of yours, you won't be surprised why you feel stuck in life because you will see how many of your thoughts are negative, self-critical, and driven by fear of the future. These thoughts can create a barrier between you and the emotional peace you desire.

You've probably come across the idea of practicing affirmations. For many, this concept can be hard to accept. Some people get turned off as soon as they hear the word "affirmations." I totally get it. Chanting "I'm a confident person" when you are actually freaking out can make you feel like a hypocrite. I've been there, trying out different affirmation techniques and sometimes feeling like I was just reciting lines. But then it hit me— *everyone is practicing affirmations throughout their life, whether they realize it or not!*

You're always thinking which means you are always affirming something to yourself. Every day, you strengthen your beliefs about yourself and the world around you. These beliefs dictate how you look at opportunities, handle challenges, and experience life. They influence your reality in ways you might not even notice. So why not use that constant thought chatter to your advantage? Every time you catch yourself in a negative thought or self-doubt mode, you can flip the script! Even if you're not fully convinced by the positive affirmations, just repeating them starts to shift your mindset.

"But what about feeling like a hypocrite?" you may ask. If repeating affirmations makes you feel odd, think about the number of times you repeat negative thoughts in your head. All I am asking you to do is repeat positive thoughts instead.

When affirmations feel like lies, remember this: your negative beliefs are just stories you've been telling yourself. They might not be true either— they're just thoughts you've accepted over time. At any moment in time, you have the freedom to pick a better narrative, a better story. Whether you go for positive affirmations or stick with negative thoughts, whatever you believe becomes your truth.

When you choose to swap out negative thoughts for positive affirmations, you actively rewire your brain. Over time, these affirmations become your new reality.

Let me give you a real-life example. Virat Kohli, one of the most successful cricketers in the world, owes his extraordinary career to the power of positive affirmations. During India's tour to Australia in the 2011-12 season, Kohli faced a significant challenge. Despite his success in One-Day Internationals, he struggled in the Test matches. Instead of letting this get him down, he turned to positive affirmations to boost his self-belief. He constantly affirmed, "I am a good enough player. I have scored 8 centuries in the one-dayers; I can score in any format." These words became his mantra, repeated both on and off the field.

This relentless self-talk helped him keep his confidence and focus, even when things weren't going his way. The turning point came in the third Test of the series. Despite failing in the first two Tests, he became the highest scorer in both innings of the third Test, proving to himself and the world that he could succeed in any format. In the fourth and final Test, he scored a remarkable century, marking a significant breakthrough in his career.

Since then, he hasn't looked back. His commitment to positive affirmations has had a tremendous impact on his performance. Virat Kohli's journey shows how powerful our thoughts can be in shaping our reality.

How Positive Affirmations Work

If you have done the work in Steps 1 and 2, you probably have identified the origin of your negative thoughts and understood their impact on your emotions. Now you need to learn to overcome these self-sabotaging thoughts. That's what affirmations are for! Affirmations are positive statements that help you challenge and overcome self-sabotaging and negative thoughts. But how do they actually work? It all comes down to how your brain processes information.

There is a part of your brain called the **Reticular Activating System (RAS)**. Think of the RAS as a filter that helps your brain decide what information to focus on. There's so much happening around you all the time, but your brain can't pay attention to everything. So, it focuses on things that seem important—based on your thoughts, experiences, and beliefs.

Here's where affirmations come in. When you repeat positive statements, like "I am confident" or "I am capable of achieving my goals," you're basically telling your RAS to start paying attention to anything that supports these beliefs. Over time, this filter begins to highlight opportunities, people, and experiences that align with your affirmations. It's not magic—it's just your brain being trained to focus on things that match the thoughts you're feeding it.

This is connected to something called the "Observational Selection Bias." Have you noticed how after you buy something, like a car, you suddenly start seeing the same car model everywhere? This is an example of **Observational Selection Bias**, which happens when your brain starts paying more attention to something after it becomes relevant to you. It's not that there are more of those cars on the road, but now that it's on your mind, your brain is selectively noticing them more often, thanks to the RAS. Similarly, affirmations tune your brain to look for things that support your positive self-talk, helping you build new thought patterns and behaviours.

So, affirmations work because they train your brain to notice more of what you're affirming, allowing you to move in the direction of your goals with greater confidence and clarity.

You've understood the science. Now what? Knowledge is great, but action is where the magic happens. So, let's learn how you can create personalized and effective affirmations.

Principles of Effective Affirmations:

1. *Clarity:* Think about the areas of your life you want to improve. Need more confidence? Better stress management? Stronger motivation? Identifying your needs will help you create clear and customized affirmations. Say your affirmations in the present tense as if they are already true. This makes them more believable. For example, say "I am" instead of "I will be." Try saying, "I will be confident." Now say. "I am confident." What feels better?

2. *Specificity:* Give your brain a specific target. General statements can be less motivating because they lack a clear vision. Instead of saying, "I am successful," say, "I am achieving my monthly sales targets." Success is a very broad term. Define what success means to you. If you say, "I am getting better," specify what "better" means and better at what. For example, "I am improving my public speaking skills" is clear and direct, making it more effective.

3. *Emotional Resonance:* Affirmations should make you feel excited. Add your emotions to make them more impactful. When you say your affirmations, feel the emotions you might feel when you achieve your goals. If you're affirming, "I am confident and capable," try to genuinely feel confident and capable as you say it. Emotional engagement makes the affirmation more powerful and helps it go deeper into your subconscious mind.

Why do you need to repeat affirmations?

You may wonder why you need to repeat them. Can't we just say them once and be done? The short answer is no. The long answer lies in the science of how our brain works.

Repetition is important for your affirmations to work their magic. A study published in *Psychological Science* discovered that repeated exposure to a statement increases the likelihood of it being perceived as true. This phenomenon is known as the **"Illusory truth effect."** Our brain is wired to believe something more readily if we hear it often enough.

You must have noticed that political campaigns often use key phrases or slogans and repeat them to make their messages more believable and memorable. During an election, a candidate might repeatedly say, "I will create jobs and reduce taxes." Over time, this constant repetition can make the statement seem more credible and convincing to the public.

Similarly, when you repeat affirmations regularly, you are essentially training your brain to accept these positive statements as truths. This is how you will stop feeling like a hypocrite when you use affirmations. Affirmations need to be a consistent part of your daily routine to be effective. By repeating affirmations, you're not just saying words; you're actively reshaping your brain's neural pathways. (remember neuroplasticity?) Over time, these new, positive pathways can replace the old, negative ones. Positive thoughts will become a habit helping you form a more optimistic mindset.

You have to give it time to work and not expect immediate results. Your negative beliefs have formed over several years, maybe decades. So, it's not fair to expect your first practice of affirmations to drastically change your life.

Integrating Affirmations into Daily Practice

If you have created your affirmations, great! If not, you can refer to the affirmations given at the end of this chapter and start your practice. Even the best intentions are useless until there is action. That's what most people including me, struggle with. Believe me, even if you are super motivated to practice your affirmations today, you might get bored after a few days, you might not feel excited or life will get in the way, and nothing will change in your life.

After a lot of trial and error, I have created a few techniques you can apply that will make it easy to be consistent with this practice. Setting aside a few minutes in the morning to practice affirmations won't make a big difference because remember, repetition is key. Most people don't have the patience for something to begin giving results. We want the results of our actions fast!

I know it's not fair but it's just the way it is, and we need to find a way to work around it. So, you need to make sure that you repeat your affirmations as much as you can during the first month of practice. You need to go all in and be obsessed with them. This is the way to bring noticeable results. When you see results, you will get the additional push and motivation to keep doing it.

Practicing affirmations for only 5-10 minutes in the morning would take a long time for them to start changing your thought patterns. Without any visible results, your mind will label it as a useless activity, prompting you to stop the practice. In short, less effort>> less results>> lesser efforts>> lesser results>> termination of effort.

Here's what you can do to get started. You can use any of the following three techniques depending on your location.

1. *Affirmation Alarm Method:*

What's the one thing you always have with you? Your phone, right? You must have a note-taking app in it. In the morning, write down 5 affirmations you want to repeat that day in that app. Set an hourly alarm throughout the day to practice your affirmation techniques for 5 minutes. Think of it as your hourly dose of positivity, like taking a vitamin but for your mind. When your hourly alarm goes off, go to your notes app and repeat the affirmations to yourself.

If you are at your workplace, you can repeat them in your mind. You may be tempted to skip the practice during work hours. But if you try it for a day, you will notice that this practice makes your workday so much better because you'll feel confident and be able to focus on your dreams and goals for which you are working. It will motivate you to work harder to achieve the goals that you are affirming.

2. *The Good News Affirmation Technique*

If you struggle with feeling the emotions while affirming, a unique and effective way to make affirmations feel more real and impactful is to say them as if you are telling them to someone else. This technique helps add an emotional touch to your affirmations.

Take your phone and pretend that you're on the phone with a friend, family member, or someone you admire. As you "speak" to them, you say your affirmation as if it has already happened to you and you are sharing the good news with them. You may say, "I got my dream job," or "I am a best-selling author," or "I just made 1 crore of revenue in my company."

Sharing good news with others, especially with people you look up to, feels great. Even if the call is imaginary, the emotions are real. You will feel proud, happy, and excited. These emotions help add more power to your affirmations. So, try it even if feels a little awkward at first. You'll gain an outside perspective, which helps bypass the self-doubt that often arises when you're repeating affirmations only to yourself.

Pro tip: If you have a close friend or family member who's also into personal growth, consider becoming affirmation buddies. Take turns sharing your good news affirmations, either in person or over the phone. Congratulate each other as you do it. It's really fun.

3. *Sticky Note Affirmation Method*

This technique is for you if you love starting your day on a positive note. To practice this technique, you will need some sticky notes and a pen. Write your affirmations on the sticky notes and place them strategically all over your house or on your work desk. This way, you will see them often. If you often struggle with maintaining consistency in your affirmation practice, this method is really useful. When you see good things written about yourself everywhere around you, it's a great boost for your self-esteem.

How to Implement the Sticky Note Affirmation Method

1. ***Create Your Affirmations:***
   - These should be positive statements that counteract any negative thoughts or limiting beliefs you might have. For example:
     - "I am confident and capable."
     - "I attract positive opportunities."
     - "I am in control of my emotions."

2. ***Write on Sticky Notes:***
   - Use colourful sticky notes to make them more eye-catching. Write one affirmation on each sticky note in bold, clear handwriting.

3. ***Place Strategically:***
   - Stick these notes in places you see often throughout your day. Ideal spots include:
     - Bathroom mirror
     - Refrigerator door
     - Computer screen
     - Inside your planner or notebook
     - On your car dashboard
     - Next to your bed
     - Above your work desk

This method is a great way to create a supportive environment that continuously encourages positive thinking.

Try each of the methods we discussed and see which one you enjoy and what works for you. Do it every single day. Remember, the power of affirmations lies in repetition. Every word you speak to yourself is a building block of your future.

Affirmations for practice:

1. **Self-love and Confidence**
   - "I am the most confident version of myself right now."
   - "I love and accept myself as I am."
   - "I trust myself to make the right decisions."

2. **Health and Well-Being**
   - "I am full of energy and vitality, ready to take on the day."
   - "I feel healthy and strong."
   - "I prioritize my health and make choices that nourish my body and mind."

3. **Career and Success**
   - "I can achieve my goals."
   - "I stay focused and succeed."
   - "Success comes to me easily."

4. **Relationships and Social Connections**
   - "I attract good people."
   - "I build strong connections."
   - "I deserve loving relationships."

5. **Wealth and Abundance**
   - "I welcome money and abundance."
   - "Money flows to me easily."
   - "I manage my finances well."

6. **Personal Growth and Learning**
   - "I learn and grow every day."
   - "I am open to new experiences."
   - "Everything is working out for me."

7. **Emotional Healing and Resilience**
   - "I control my emotions."
   - "I let go of the past."
   - "I get stronger with every challenge."

8. **Spirituality and Inner Peace**
   - "I trust the universe."
   - "I find peace in the present."
   - "I grow spiritually every day."

9. **Creativity and Passion**
   - "I am creative and inspired."
   - "I follow my passions."
   - "My creativity flows freely."

10. **Gratitude and Mindfulness**
    - "I am grateful for my life."
    - "I enjoy the present moment."
    - "I appreciate all I have."

Chapter - 14
Rewiring Your Brain With Gratitude

"Gratitude is an antidote to negative emotions, a neutralizer of envy, hostility, worry, and irritation. It is savouring; it is not taking things for granted; it is present-oriented." – **Sonja Lyubomirsky.**

One of the fastest ways to shift your emotions is gratitude. A popular practice is making a list of things to be grateful for. But to be honest, just jotting down a daily list of things you're thankful for can feel like a chore. So, if you are not a fan of writing things to be grateful for, that's fine. In this chapter, I am going to share some fun and engaging ways to make gratitude a delightful part of daily routine. But first, let's understand why gratitude is such a big deal.

In 2004, psychologists Christopher Peterson and Martin Seligman published a book called "Character Strengths and Virtues: A Handbook and Classification." They listed 24 character strengths grouped into six virtues. Guess which strength was the best predictor of well-being? Gratitude!

> *Just being grateful for what you have can flip negative emotions into positive ones. It's the exact opposite of complaining. Most of our negative thoughts are just us complaining about something. It's impossible to be grateful and complain at the same time. Gratitude is the antidote to negative thinking.*

When you consistently practice gratitude, you create new neural pathways that rewire your thought patterns. Gratitude activates the brain's reward system by boosting dopamine (the pleasure and motivation chemical) and serotonin (the happiness and relaxation chemical). A 2017 analysis of 38 studies found that gratitude practices improved well-being, happiness, and life satisfaction while cutting down depressive symptoms.

Gratitude can add years to your life. Studies show that people who regularly practice gratitude have better sleep quality, lower blood pressure, less inflammation, and are less likely to engage in unhealthy habits like smoking or excessive drinking. It's natural, isn't it? When you appreciate your body, you're less likely to harm it with toxins.

Do You Find It Hard to Be Grateful?

Research on twins has shown that genetics can play a role in how naturally grateful we are. For example, identical twins, who share the same DNA, often report similar levels of gratitude. In contrast, fraternal twins, who only share half their DNA, tend to have more differences in how grateful they feel.

One gene called COMT affects how dopamine, a feel-good chemical in the brain, is recycled. People with certain versions of this gene might naturally feel more grateful, while others with different versions might find it harder to feel grateful and may be more sensitive to negative events. This means that some of our ability to feel gratitude could be inherited, which might explain why it's easier for some people and harder for others.

While these genes can influence how grateful you naturally are, it doesn't mean you cannot become more grateful. That's why gratitude practices exist. So, you too can reap the benefits of gratitude, but they might not be immediate. For some, it may take two to three weeks to notice improvements in their physical and emotional well-being.

People often miss out on these benefits because they have high expectations that aren't quickly met. If you're dealing with severe depression or anxiety, expecting that gratitude practices will suddenly make everything better might lead to disappointment and you might give up before you see any results.

Another reason people find it difficult to practice gratitude is that they don't live in the present moment. Gratitude is the result of awareness of our blessings. We can be aware of our blessings only if we are not lost in our own thoughts.

Some people want to start a gratitude practice but procrastinate or find it hard to make it stick. If you are one of those who find it difficult to incorporate this practice into your life, let's learn some fun and practical ways to make gratitude your default mode of thinking.

Practical Exercises

1. The Gratitude Bracelet: A Simple Yet Powerful Practice

To help you stay consistently grateful, I've designed a simple method using a special bracelet. This bracelet will remind you to focus on the positive aspects of your life all day long. Here's how to practice this:

i. Choose Your Bracelet

Pick a bracelet that you like and feel connected to. It could be a simple band that means something special to you. The idea is to choose something you enjoy wearing so that it becomes a pleasant reminder of your gratitude practice.

ii. Start Your Day with Gratitude

Every morning, wear your gratitude bracelet and take a moment to think of three things that you are grateful for. It could be something as simple as your morning coffee, a friend who's always there for you, or the fact that you have a house to live in. Starting your day with this ritual gets you into a positive mindset and sets the stage for a great day ahead.

iii. Keep it going

Throughout the day, whenever you catch sight of or feel your bracelet, use it as a reminder to think of three more things you're thankful for. Maybe it's the amazing lunch you just had, a compliment from a coworker, or that there was no traffic on your way to work. This way, you also become more mindful of the blessings around you that you may not have noticed otherwise.

iv. End the day on a high note

At the end of the day, take off your bracelet and place it on your nightstand. Spend a moment thinking about the best thing that happened during the day. Ending your day with a dose of positive reflection helps you sleep better.

The advantage of this practice is that you don't have to set aside a specific time. You don't need a reminder because your bracelet is right there on your hand, reminding you to be more present and appreciate the good things in your life. So, get yourself a bracelet and make gratitude as natural as breathing.

2. Mental subtraction technique:

There are two ways to think about the good things in your life:

1. **Presence of the Event:** For example, "I'm grateful for my car."

2. **Absence of the Event:** For example, "Imagine if I didn't have my car."

The first way is the regular "count your blessings" way. One should be grateful for having a nice house, a great husband, a good family, etc. However, humans tend to adapt to familiar things. We might feel grateful for the good things in our lives for a while. But soon, we start taking them for granted. Research shows that when we think about an event often, it starts to feel more familiar and easier to understand. This works well when it comes to negative events because we need to adapt quickly and move on. However, this same familiarity can also reduce the positive feelings we have about good things in our lives.

For example, you might not feel as excited about your job or a close friendship as you once did, simply because you've gotten used to them. As a result, just thinking about the positive things in your life may not bring the same emotional boost it once did.

Now, how do we "unadapt" to positive events? The second way of being grateful for positive things is to imagine what would happen if they were not there in your life. A study found that when people took time to think about how certain positive life events might never have happened, they experienced an increase in positive emotions. Because it made these events feel more special and meaningful. For example, imagine if you didn't have easy access to drinking water in your house and you had to walk miles for it. Do you feel significantly grateful toward this facility in your house now? Do you notice the difference between thinking "I'm grateful for having easy access to drinking water," and thinking "What if I didn't have easy access to drinking water?"

Researchers called this the "George Bailey effect." There is an old classic film called "It's a Wonderful Life." You must have heard of it. It was released in 1946. In the film, an angel named Clarence Odbody comes to rescue a suicidal man named George Bailey. Before George can jump into the river, Clarence dives into the freezing river and George rescues him. Out of despair, George expresses that he should have never been born. Clarence then decides to show George what would have happened if George never existed. As a 12-year-old, George had rescued his younger brother Harry from drowning. But since he didn't exist, George discovers Harry's grave. In the past, George had saved a pharmacist, Mr. Gower, from accidentally poisoning a customer. But in this new world without him, he finds Mr. Gower jailed for manslaughter because George was not there to stop him from poisoning the customer. He later visits his mom and wife, but both of them don't recognize him. When George views the world without the most important blessings of his life, he begs for his life back. He realizes just how much the people around him needed him and how much he missed his old life.

When you think about your life without your current blessings, it can help you undo adaptation to them, at least temporarily. Dutch psychologist Nico Frijda explains that we can prevent ourselves from getting too used to good things by regularly reminding ourselves of how lucky we are. By reflecting on how our situation could have been different or worse, or how it was in the past, we can keep feeling grateful and appreciate what we have through memory and imagination.

You don't need to wait for an angel to show you what the world would look like if you had never been born. Instead, you can look around and imagine your life without all that surrounds you so that you can truly appreciate your life for what it is.

Practical Exercise: The Mental Subtraction Technique

Step 1: Identify a Positive Aspect of Your Life

1. Think about a specific positive event, person, or achievement in your life that you are grateful for. For example: A supportive friend, a job you love, a memorable trip.

Write down the positive aspect you have chosen:

_____

_____

Step 2: Imagine Its Absence

2. Reflect on how different your life would be if this positive aspect had never occurred or if this person were not in your life.

Describe how your life would be without this positive aspect:

_____

_____

_____

Step 3: Appreciate the Present

3. Now, focus on your current life and how this positive aspect contributes to it.

   - Think about the joy, support, or benefits it brings you.
   - Reflect on why you are grateful to have this positive aspect in your life.

Write down your thoughts and feelings about having this positive aspect in your life now:

_____

_____

Chapter - 15
You Daily Emotional Detox

"Values are related to our emotions, just as we practice physical hygiene to preserve our physical health, we need to observe emotional hygiene to preserve a healthy mind and attitudes." **- Dalai Lama.**

There was this one day when I was so overwhelmed with my emotions that I couldn't even pinpoint what I was feeling. I couldn't put a name to the emotion. So, I opened up my journal app (I use Day One) and just started writing. I needed to let it all out and I poured out everything I'd felt in the past year—the mistakes, the frustrations, the vulnerable moments, feelings of unworthiness, and even the emotions I wasn't proud of.

In the middle of this emotional release, I was taken aback by how much I'd been holding in and hiding, even from myself. I wasn't writing to find a solution. The solution was to offload these feelings somewhere. Once I was done, it felt like a massive weight had been lifted off my shoulders. Looking at the mess of my emotions, I thought I'd judge myself harshly. But I didn't. I realized that these thoughts weren't me. It was as if I'd separated them from my mind by writing them down and giving them a new place to exist. Their new home was my journal, not my mind. So, the moment I wrote them down, those feelings no longer felt like they were a part of me. It's amazing how therapeutic it can be to just let it all out. It gave me the courage to start with a fresh mindset. I had shed my past and was free from its chains, which meant I was free to make new choices from then on.

You cannot put a stopper on your emotions without causing problems in your life. They manifest in the form of outbursts of anger, exaggerated reactions to something trivial, making a big deal out of nothing, trying to find faults in others or needing to feel superior to others to maintain our self-worth.

Yet we keep loading new emotions on top of the older unreleased ones which causes our perception of the world to get blurrier. If we take the time to practice emotional hygiene by writing our feelings somewhere we can make space in our minds for cultivating new positive emotions.

You know that you need to feel positive to attract positive things in your life, but you are unable to do it beyond a certain point, and it almost feels fake if you try too hard. The reason is simple. There is no space for new positive emotions in your mind. You can create this space by creating a ritual of daily emotional detox. It's like free therapy, and if you do it every night imagine the kind of sleep you will be getting. You won't need to think about the things that happened in the past or during the day because you would have already released them from your mind.

Let's see how to do this. You simply need to take a journal and write down every emotion you felt during the day. Don't judge and restrict yourself. Even if you acted in ways that made you feel ashamed of yourself, just get it down on paper. It's difficult to face your dark side. Getting it on paper can feel like you're a bad person and you're making it official by writing it down. But remember you are simply becoming aware of yourself and your patterns so that you can pinpoint what is holding you back. Awareness is the first step towards a positive change.

After you are done, write or say this statement aloud: **These thoughts are not me and I am now releasing them and creating more space in my mind for new positive thoughts.**

This process is more than just journaling. In regular journaling, you might write about your day, and your experiences, and reflect on them. But here, you're not just documenting events—you're actively releasing emotions. The goal isn't to go into the details of your day or note down trivial moments. Instead, it's about bringing your emotions to the surface without judgment and then consciously letting them go. It's a practice of emotional detox, not just reflection.

Benefits of This Practice:

1. *Improved mood and decreased stress:* Spending even 10 minutes writing down your feelings each day can improve your mood and reduce stress.

2. *Better relationships:* You're less likely to project your negativity onto others if you have a way of releasing it on your own. Relationships, whether with family, friends, or colleagues, are all about what you bring to the table, and when you practice emotional detox, you create a peaceful and positive space for those relationships to thrive. It's normal to want to vent out to others when something is bothering you, but it's important to recognize that not every negative emotion needs to be shared.

   First, you need to take responsibility for your emotional well-being. After processing your emotions on your own, if you still feel the need to talk to somebody, that's okay. In fact, if you do this practice, you'll become more aware of your emotions and be able to clearly communicate your feelings to other people. This can help them help you in a better way.

3. *Increased emotional awareness:* This practice helps you identify and understand your feelings better which can help you find the root cause of the pain you are feeling. So, you're addressing emotional pain rather than ignoring it, which is great for your mental health.

The practice of daily emotional detox is a powerful tool for personal growth and mental health. It allows us to confront our emotions, understand them, and ultimately, let them go. It creates space in your mind for new, positive thoughts and emotions and is a form of self-therapy that can lead to profound changes in your life.

Practical Exercise: Daily Emotional Detox Worksheet

Here's a worksheet that you can use to release your emotions each night:

1. **How are you feeling right now?** *(Circle all that apply)*
   - Happy
   - Sad
   - Angry
   - Anxious
   - Stressed
   - Calm
   - Grateful
   - Frustrated
   - Excited
   - Other:

2. **Events of the Day**
   - **What happened today that might have influenced your emotions?**

   (List key events or interactions)
   - _____
   - _____
   - _____

3. **Releasing Emotions**
   - **What emotions do you want to release tonight?**

   (Write down any emotions that are weighing you down)
   - _____
   - _____
   - _____

- _____
- _____
- _____

4. **Reflecting on Positive Moments**
   - **What positive or uplifting moments did you experience today?**

   (List moments that made you feel good)

   - _____
   - _____
   - _____

   - **How did these moments make you feel?**

   (Write a few sentences about your emotions during these positive experiences)

   - _____
   - _____
   - _____

5. **Setting an Intention for Tomorrow**
   - **What emotion or mindset do you want to carry into tomorrow?**

   (Choose one or more intentions)

   - Calmness
   - Positivity
   - Gratitude
   - Patience
   - Confidence
   - Other: _____

   - **Write a short affirmation or intention for tomorrow:**

- _____
- _____
- _____

6. *Visualization*
   - **Take a few moments to visualize releasing the emotions you've identified.**

   (Imagine them washing away, leaving you feeling lighter and more at peace)

   - How do you feel after this visualization?

_____
_____
_____
_____

⟨⊗⟩

Step - 4
REBUILD
Build Resilience and Inner Strength

When we experience trauma or deep emotional pain, it can feel like our world is falling apart. But it's also an opportunity for us to rebuild. This process of rebuilding often makes us stronger and more resilient. It's like a muscle that gets stronger each time it's used.

In this step, we will discuss how to build resilience and understand the importance of social support. We will also learn how trauma can be a blessing, how to find meaning in suffering and learn how to solve problems in life using a pragmatic approach.

Chapter - 16
What Is Resilience?

*"Resilience is knowing that you are the only one that has the power and the responsibility to pick yourself up." – **Mary Holloway.***

Did you have one of those inflatable bouncy toys as a kid? The kind that, no matter how hard you punched it, would pop right back up? That's the perfect way to understand resilience. Life might knock us down a hundred times, but we have the ability to bounce back. Emotional resilience doesn't mean we won't experience difficulties. It means that even if we lose our emotional balance, we know how to find our way back home to our true nature of peace, joy, and calm.

To build yourself up again, you need to develop resilience. Even if you think you are not a naturally strong person, or you have no energy left after going through a tough situation, understand this: Resilience isn't something we're born with; it's a skill we can develop, like everything else in life. Remember neuroplasticity? It's the brain's ability to reorganize itself by forming new neural connections. It plays an important role in building resilience. With the right tools and effort, you can become a more resilient person.

The Impact of Early Life Experiences

Moderate Adversity in Childhood

If you faced struggles early in life, you might be surprised to learn that research suggests people who experience moderate adversity during childhood often develop stronger resilience compared to those who face none. This is because overcoming difficulties helps build self-confidence and adaptability. This is called the "steeling effect," where overcoming challenges strengthens a person's ability to deal with future challenges.

Moderate adversity, in this sense, serves as a kind of mental and emotional training ground.

If you experienced moderate stress during your childhood, you might feel bad that your childhood was tough. But knowing that it made you more capable of handling the challenges you may be facing now, I don't think you would want to change anything that happened in your life. As tough as they were, your challenges helped you build the inner strength you now have, and this steeling effect has helped you develop a mental toughness that can continue to serve you well in adulthood.

Severe Adversity in Childhood

It's important to understand that resilience develops when stress is *moderate*, not extreme. Severe or chronic stress, such as enduring prolonged neglect, physical or emotional abuse, or exposure to violence, can overwhelm a child's developing brain and nervous system. In such cases, the stress-response system becomes overactive, leading to what is known as "toxic stress."

Unlike moderate stress, which builds resilience, toxic stress can damage areas of the brain responsible for regulating emotions, memory, and decision-making. As a result, people who experience severe adversity may struggle with anxiety, depression, and difficulty managing their stress when they reach adulthood.

If your childhood was marked by extreme stress, you may feel more vulnerable to anxiety, depression, or feeling "stuck" in negative patterns. You may start feeling sorry for yourself which will push you into the role of the victim. Being a victim means you'll be stuck in a place of powerlessness, feeling like life is happening *to* you. It's not a great place to be in even if it feels safe. Just because you are tired doesn't mean you need to give your power away.

Now that you recognize that childhood adversity might be the root cause of your anxiety and depression, you can take steps to heal. You may not be able to change your childhood, but you can look at it with more compassion. Resilience is not only built through overcoming challenges; it also grows through self-compassion. You need to be kind to yourself for surviving difficult experiences without feeling sorry for yourself.

> *When you acknowledge your pain without allowing it to define you, you shift from being a victim to being a survivor. And when you start giving yourself the time and space to heal and rebuild yourself, you step into the role of a warrior.*

You cannot let your past dictate your future any longer than you already have. You have the same ability as other people to develop a stronger version of yourself.

The Science of Healing from Childhood Stress

Research shows that childhood trauma can affect brain development, particularly in areas that regulate emotions and stress. But now you know that your brain has the ability to change and adapt. This means that, even if early adversity wired your brain to be more anxious or reactive, you can now rewire it for resilience and emotional stability.

Studies have shown that practices like mindfulness, exercise, therapy, and even positive social interactions can help rebuild the brain's capacity to handle stress more effectively. **The most important takeaway from this book is that you don't have to live with the emotional patterns your childhood created.** With effort, patience, and self-compassion, you can create new patterns of strength and resilience.

Broaden and Build Theory for Building Resilience

According to psychologist Barbara Fredrickson, positive emotions like joy, gratitude, and love help build resilience. She put forth a simple theory called the "Broaden and Build Theory". When we feel positive emotions our minds "broaden," meaning we think more openly and creatively. We're more willing to try new things, explore different ideas, and connect with others. You must have experienced this yourself. When you are happy, you are more likely to take on challenges. When you are in a bad mood, you tend to say no to the things you once used to enjoy. This is because negative emotions narrow your focus. Even though they have an important role to play, nurturing them drains your energy and puts you in a defensive state where you're just trying to survive the moment.

Positive emotions are like sources of energy. As we experience more positive emotions and broaden our thinking, we start to "build" lasting resources. It's like storing food in preparation for bad weather conditions. Tough times can appear out of nowhere. You need to build your mental storehouse with resources like skills, knowledge, stronger relationships, or even better health. These resources act as a support system that you can use when life throws challenges your way.

For instance, the friendships you build when you're feeling happy can support you during tough times. The skills you learn when you're feeling motivated can become the tools you rely on when life gets tough. So, positive emotions are not just fleeting experiences—they are the building blocks of resilience.

The key takeaway from Fredrickson's theory is that if we cultivate more positive emotions, we can improve our ability to handle life's ups and downs. And you're already on your way to doing that if you have started implementing the tools in Step 3. These tools that help you think positively are also the tools that make you a stronger person who can withstand all kinds of stress in life. As you continue to broaden your mind with positive experiences, you'll naturally build up a set of resources that you can lean on when times get tough.

Broaden and Build for Everyday Life

To put this theory into practice, start by seeking out small ways to create positive emotions in your daily life. (Refer step 3: REFRAME) It could be something as simple as going for a walk in nature, taking a few moments to appreciate something beautiful, or spending time with a loved one. These small actions broaden your perspective and help you build the emotional strength necessary to handle stress.

Chapter - 17
Social Support: Your Key To Resilience

At times our own light goes out and is rekindled by a spark from another person. Each of us has cause to think with deep gratitude of those who have lighted the flame within us. – Albert Schweitzer

We discussed that going through adversity in childhood can make you more resilient in the future. But how does it happen? If you want to understand it, think of a seesaw.

When positive experiences outweigh negative experiences, the "scale" tips toward positive outcomes

If you face adversity as a child, there should be enough positive experiences on one side to counterbalance significant adversity on the other. Resilience develops when the positive experiences outweigh the negative ones. That's when the "scale" tips toward positive outcomes. One of the things that helps the scale tip toward positive outcomes is supportive relationships with your parents, family members, or teachers. Positive relationships absorb the impact of stress on the child. As a child, if you felt supported and understood, you are more likely to develop a strong sense of self-worth. It makes you believe that you can overcome obstacles.

Just like positive relationships help a child withstand stress, people with strong social networks are better able to recover from stress and tough times. However, not everyone naturally has the traits that make it easy to build such a network. If you're an introvert like me, you might worry that you're at a disadvantage because you prefer solitude and may not have a large circle of friends to lean on during challenging times. You may not have the energy to make such connections. You might also question if it's really worth your time and effort. Don't give it to these thoughts that make you stuck in your comfort zone.

I used to believe that I didn't need anyone until I met my extroverted husband. I understood how easy life can be when you have supportive relationships and getting help from others is not something to be ashamed of. He often reminds me of a line from *How I Met Your Mother*, one of those classic Barney Stinson quotes: *"Whatever you do in this life, it's not legendary unless your friends are there to see it."*

No matter who you are, you need other people. Sure, you may not need a large social circle, but it's essential to have your own small tribe.

Your tribe is the people who are happy for you when you share your achievements, people who give you honest feedback, call you out when you are going in the wrong direction, provide different perspectives to your problems, and support you when your motivation wanes. Having a close-knit group of people, you can rely on makes all the difference in navigating life's ups and downs.

It's not just introverts who need to be intentional about this; extroverts, too, can benefit from learning how to cultivate a strong, supportive social network. If you are an extrovert, you may find it easier to connect with others, but you also need to be careful about who has access to you. You need to identify people who contribute something to your life and form quality relationships that can provide true support when it's needed most. So, whether you're an introvert or an extrovert, building a strong network is essential, and it's something that can be learned and developed by anyone.

How to build your social support network

1. **Quality Over Quantity:** Having a large group of friends hinders the ability to make deep connections as you practically cannot spend one-on-one time with a large group. A few deep, meaningful friendships are more than enough for emotional support. It's a good idea to join hobby clubs where you can effortlessly find people who share your interests.

2. **Leverage Existing Relationships:** Often while pursuing other goals in life, we grow apart from old friends. For introverts, it's even harder to make new connections. So, you don't need to start from scratch. Strengthening bonds with people you already know, and trust can be a great way to build support. Reach out to a close friend or family member and schedule regular check-ins, whether through phone calls, video chats, or in-person meetings.

3. **Use your strengths:** Being an introvert comes with unique strengths that can be incredibly valuable in creating your tribe. Your ability to let the other person talk and listen deeply helps you form deep, meaningful connections. You can make people feel safe when they share their deepest thoughts because they know you're selective when it comes to making friends and won't gossip about them to random people.

   Extroverts, on the other hand, are great at initiating interactions and bringing energy to social settings. As an extrovert, you can use your natural enthusiasm to create a welcoming environment and connect with others quickly. By leveraging these strengths, you can build and nurture supportive relationships.

4. **Stay True to Yourself:** Authenticity is important in any relationship. You want people to like you for who you are. You

will be saving a lot of your time if you are genuine as it will attract the right people into your life who appreciate and support you as you are.

5. **Give and Take:** A strong network is built on reciprocity. Be there for others when they need support, and don't hesitate to ask for help when you need it.

Building and maintaining supportive networks is not just beneficial but essential for emotional well-being whether you accept it or not. With no one to share our thoughts with, our thoughts can begin to dominate our minds. They can often mislead us. When we talk to our friends about a problem we are facing, they often give you perspectives you couldn't imagine yourself. Shining a light on your problem from a different direction can sometimes show you the exact solution.

However, you must learn to process your emotions before talking to someone you can trust. Knowing that someone is there to listen and provide comfort makes challenges feel more manageable. They might share their own stories of struggle which can help you feel less alone. Even if you don't talk to them, observing how strong people tackle tough times can help you learn how to cope, adapt, and thrive.

Whether you are an introvert or an extrovert, feeling connected to others is a fundamental human need. Positive people can change your perspective by encouraging you, highlighting your strengths, and reminding you of your past successes. This positive reinforcement builds your confidence in overcoming challenges.

Should you cut off "toxic" relationships?

You might see many posts on social media about toxic friends and how to spot them. But it's important to understand that people are complex, and no one is entirely good or bad. Labelling is a cognitive distortion, remember? It reduces a person to a single negative trait. At some point in life, we are all "toxic" to someone.

People might act in ways that are harmful due to stress, trauma, or personal struggles, but that doesn't mean their entire identity is toxic. When someone is labelled as toxic, the immediate response is often to cut ties. It can cause relationships to end prematurely without trying to address the issues. This whole thing about "cutting toxic people off" gives the wrong idea that people are disposable. It's important to give people the chance to change or adjust before writing them off completely.

Instead of labelling someone as toxic, you can try focusing on specific behaviours that you must not tolerate and use that awareness to set up boundaries. This allows you to protect your emotional health while also leaving room for change and growth in the relationship.

Signs of Unhealthy Behaviour:

1. **Constant Negativity:** They often criticize, judge, complain, or make you feel inferior. You feel extremely tired after talking to them. You start doubting your abilities when you're with them.

2. **Lack of Reciprocity:** They want you to be there for you, but you don't feel that you can ask for the same from them. They don't create that level of comfort for you to be able to ask for their help. You get the vibe that they're simply using you until it's convenient for them.

3. **Manipulation:** They may use guilt or pressure to control your decisions, making you feel responsible for their happiness or problems.

4. **Disrespecting Boundaries:** They don't respect your personal space, time, or feelings. It shows a lack of care for your well-being.

While supportive relationships make you resilient and strong, unhealthy relationships can do the opposite. While building your tribe, you must be aware of people who drain your energy and don't add anything valuable to your life. Just because they were a part of your life for a long time doesn't mean you have to be friends with them forever, especially if all they do is try to bring you down. Rather than cutting ties immediately, you might first try setting clear boundaries.

How to Set Healthy Boundaries:

- **Communicate your needs clearly:** Let your friends know when something they do makes you uncomfortable. For example: "I feel uncomfortable when you criticize me constantly. I need us to focus on more positive conversations."

- **Take small steps:** You don't need to end a friendship abruptly. Start by reducing time spent together or having more emotionally neutral interactions.

- **Respect your limits:** If a friend repeatedly crosses your boundaries, you may need to reassess the role they play in your life.

As an introvert, I have a few friends but all of them are genuine. I am very thankful to my friends who accept me as I am. I am not always up for going out to a party, I can sometimes act distant or be lost in my own world. Some of my behaviours could also be labelled as "toxic" but thankfully my friends chose to see the whole of me and not just the toxic behaviour. They gave me a chance to change and grow. It helped me a lot in becoming a good friend to them. They didn't give up on me and I'm forever grateful to them for that. I want you to look at your friends the same way.

So, remember, not all friendships are perfect, and challenging relationships can sometimes grow stronger with clear communication and boundaries. Instead of seeing someone as "toxic," it's often better to recognize problematic behaviours while giving space for growth and change. Only if the negativity persists despite your efforts should you consider distancing yourself.

Practical Exercise: The Support Network Map

- **Objective**: Identify and strengthen your existing support system.
- **Steps**:

1. Draw a circle in the middle of a page and write your name on it.
2. Around the circle, draw smaller circles representing the people who play significant roles in your life (family, friends, colleagues, mentors, etc.).
3. Draw lines connecting your circle to the smaller circles, indicating the strength of your relationship (thicker lines for stronger connections).
4. Reflect on which connections you can strengthen. Identify at least one person you can reach out to more often or spend quality time with.
5. Create an action plan to nurture these connections (e.g., schedule regular calls, plan meet-ups, or engage in shared activities)

Chapter - 18
Trauma Can Be A Blessing

"Rock bottom became the solid foundation on which I rebuilt my life."
– J.K. Rowling.

Post-Traumatic Growth

Healing from emotional trauma starts when you choose a new direction that takes you away from old wounds and negative patterns. Many of us think that emotional trauma makes us weak, but did you know that there exists something called **Post-Traumatic Growth**? It's a positive psychological change that some people go through after a crisis or a traumatic event. It doesn't mean that they didn't feel hurt by the events. They got deeply hurt but going through the event made them stronger and gave them certain skills, almost like getting power-ups after completing a level in a video game.

Post-Traumatic Growth vs. Resilience

Post-traumatic growth (PTG) differs from resilience, although the two are often linked. Resilience refers to the ability to bounce back from adversity, to regain balance after life's challenges. It's about returning to a baseline of functioning. Post-traumatic growth, on the other hand, is about transformation. This term was coined by psychologists Richard Tedeschi and Lawrence Calhoun. They observed that those who experience PTG don't just return to their previous state of being—they evolve into a new version of themselves. The trauma acts as a turning point that leads to deeper personal growth, a stronger sense of purpose, and a more profound appreciation for life.

Many survivors of severe trauma, like army veterans or people who have experienced major natural disasters, report feeling a profound transformation after enduring such challenges. For example, after

Hurricane Katrina, survivors who lost their homes and livelihoods often described a renewed sense of purpose. Many went on to volunteer and help rebuild their communities. One woman, who lost everything, shared how she initially felt broken but eventually saw the disaster as a "second chance" at life—an opportunity to reconnect with what truly mattered to her: her family, her neighbours, and her sense of community.

The Five Pathways of Post-Traumatic Growth

Research has identified five main ways that people experience PTG:

1. **New Opportunities:** Survivors of trauma often develop a new perspective on life, which allows them to seek out new opportunities. The traumatic experience can act as a wake-up call, making them more open to change and growth.

2. **Stronger Relationships:** Those who experience PTG often form more meaningful and resilient relationships, not just with loved ones but also with others who have faced similar struggles.

3. **Increased Inner Strength:** Overcoming trauma helps people realize they are far stronger than they once believed. This realization can increase their self-confidence and courage when facing future challenges.

4. **A Deeper Appreciation for Life:** Trauma often shifts one's values, leading to a deeper appreciation for life's simple moments. Survivors may develop a stronger sense of gratitude for the things they once took for granted.

5. **Spiritual and Existential Growth:** Experiences of trauma frequently lead to changes in one's worldview, including a re-evaluation of religious or spiritual beliefs. They can feel a deeper sense of connection to something greater than oneself, whether that be through faith, philosophy, or a sense of life's purpose.

The author of **The Miracle Morning, Hal Elrod** is a remarkable example of Post-Traumatic Growth (PTG). In 1999, he was a 20-year-old successful sales representative. One night, while driving home, he was hit head-on by a drunk driver at 70 miles per hour. The impact was so severe that his car spun off the road and was hit again by another vehicle. Hal was clinically dead for six minutes. He suffered 11 broken bones and permanent brain damage, and doctors told him he might never walk again.

Though he faced the potential of permanent disability, Hal chose to focus not on what he had lost but on what he still had. He decided to become the most grateful person there could be. He applied the lessons he had learned from personal development to his healing process. Through this, not only did he defy the doctors' predictions by walking again, but he also transformed his life in ways he hadn't imagined before the accident.

This led him to develop "The Miracle Morning," a daily routine that focuses on six practices: Silence, Affirmations, Visualization, Exercise, Reading, and Scribing (writing). These practices were born out of his journey of recovery and growth after the accident.

Hal Elrod is now a globally renowned author, speaker, and personal development leader. His bestselling book, *The Miracle Morning: The Not-So-Obvious Secret Guaranteed to Transform Your Life (Before 8 AM)*, has sold over 3 million copies worldwide and has been translated into more than 30 languages. What started as his personal routine to rebuild his life has now evolved into the *Miracle Morning* movement, embraced by millions of people across the globe. Rather than returning to his pre-accident self, Hal's journey of recovery led him to create a worldwide movement through his books and teachings, influencing millions of lives.

The challenges you face don't have to be something that breaks you. Instead, they can be the very thing that unlocks your next level of growth, helping you become a more resilient, more fulfilled version of yourself.

Often, trauma forces us to question everything we thought we knew, and it's in those questions where real growth happens. Trying to make sense of difficult experiences can shift your thought patterns and challenge your old beliefs, creating space for new ways of thinking and living.

Circumstances can sometimes shake your core to bring up a new updated version of you by forcing you to see yourself, your relationships, and the world in a new light.

I hope this helps you understand the potential of your misery. Seriously, why not make use of negative situations for your own positive transformation? It's an opportunity you must not turn down.

Find Meaning in Suffering

This is another way of growing through trauma. Viktor Frankl was a psychiatrist and neurologist, who was imprisoned in the Nazi concentration camp of Auschwitz during World War II. He lost his parents, brother, and pregnant wife in the Holocaust. Any person could have crumbled under these unimaginable horrors of the camps. Yet he didn't stop learning from his situation. He observed that survival often depended not just on physical strength but on one's ability to find meaning, even in the most desperate situations. His observation was spot on, and modern research supports this as well. A 2010 study published in *Applied Psychology* showed that people with a sense of purpose tend to live longer. They also experience good health like fewer strokes and heart attacks, better sleep, and a lower risk of dementia.

Frankl noticed that those who survived the longest were often **those who had something to live for**—whether it was a loved one, a task they felt compelled to complete, or a cause they believed in. This made him develop *logotherapy*. In simple words, logotherapy says that the search for meaning is the primary motivation in life. Other psychological approaches suggest that a human being is motivated by pleasure or power. Logotherapy says that the most important drive behind our actions is the need to find meaning in life.

Frankl believed that even in the face of suffering, finding a sense of purpose can provide people with the strength to endure and overcome their circumstances. It makes sense, doesn't it? Life can feel empty and meaningless when you don't have any goals. But having goals that excite you makes life interesting and worth living. We all need a strong reason to wake up each morning. I'm not talking about goals that society has set for you, like going to work, running a business, or making money—those are necessary, but there's more to it. I'm talking about a deeper purpose, something that's uniquely yours to fulfil, something that keeps you going no matter what life throws at you. It's the pursuit of this purpose that makes life truly meaningful and beautiful.

Even in the most challenging circumstances, you have the freedom to choose your attitude. This freedom is what allows you to find meaning in suffering and transform it into a source of inner strength. It may not come naturally to many of us. So, we need to understand how it can be done in a practical way.

Frankl proposed that meaning can be found in three ways:

1. *Through work or a task:* Doing something significant, creating something, or accomplishing a goal. Even when you are going through miserable situations, you can choose to focus your attention on your goals. If you don't feel motivated enough to do that, you might have chosen the wrong goals. The right goals are those that you choose for yourself and not the ones meant to impress other people. If you have chosen the right goals, you will feel compelled to pursue them no matter what. A person can only focus on one thing at a time. Choosing to divert your attention to your goals instead of your suffering can help you overcome your suffering.

2. *Through love:* Experiencing something or someone fully, especially through relationships with others. Love has the power to heal. Loving something or someone deeply helps you connect with the source of energy you may be lacking in yourself. Have you experienced how light it feels when you share your feelings with your loved ones? Just the act of voicing it out to a trusted friend can help you find solutions.

3. *Through suffering:* Stoic philosophy says that while we may not have control over external events, we do have control over our reactions to them. Accepting this can help us endure our challenges in peace. If someone wants to hurt you, you cannot control what they may say or do to you. But there is peace in knowing that you can control your attitude because no one has access to your mind and what you can think. As the Japanese author, Haruki Murakami said, while we cannot avoid pain, how

we choose to respond to it—whether we suffer from it or not—is within our control.

Practical Exercises:

1. Rewrite your trauma story
Objective:

This exercise is designed to help you reframe your trauma by shifting your focus from pain to growth. By rewriting your story, you can uncover the strengths, lessons, and positive changes that have emerged from your experience.

Step 1: Write Your Trauma Story

Write down your trauma story, describing how the experience negatively impacted you.

Prompt:
What is my trauma story?

Step 2: Rewriting for Growth

Now, rewrite your trauma story, focusing on how it contributed to your personal growth. Think about the lessons you've learned, the strengths you've developed, and the ways you've become a stronger person.

How can I rewrite this story to highlight my personal growth?

Step 3: Reflect on Your Gains

Identify the positive changes you've experienced as a result of overcoming this trauma.

What have I gained from this experience?

_____
_____
_____
_____
_____

Source:

Adapted from the concept of Post-Traumatic Growth (PTG), first introduced by psychologists Richard Tedeschi and Lawrence Calhoun in 1996.

2. **Helping Others Through Your Experience:**

Instructions:

- Consider how your suffering could be used to help others.
- Write down at least three ways you could use your experiences to support, guide, or inspire someone else who is going through a similar situation.
- If possible, take action on one of these ideas, such as writing a supportive letter, volunteering, or sharing your story with others.

    Purpose: This exercise emphasizes the idea that meaning can often be found by helping others through your own experiences, transforming personal suffering into a source of strength and compassion.

Chapter - 19
Use Pragmatism To Solve Problems

"The pragmatist turns the spotlight on what works, not on what should work." – **William James.**

Resilience comes from the ability to quickly solve problems and keep moving forward in life. However, the goal is not to have a problem-free life. Unless you decide to live in a closed chamber, it is impossible to have a life devoid of any problems. The goal is to use your problems to upgrade yourself. So instead of trying to avoid them, it's wiser to develop a method that helps you solve them quickly and effectively.

Self-Efficacy

The first thing you need is the belief in your ability to overcome your challenges. This is called self-efficacy, and it's closely linked to resilience. Research shows that people with high self-efficacy are more likely to take proactive steps to overcome challenges, which makes them more resilient. Math teachers say the more problems you solve the better will be your ability to solve any problem. The same applies to life too. When you can solve one problem, you gain the confidence to solve other problems too. In 1998 a scientist named Carver noted that going through tough experiences can make you less affected by future difficulties, similar to how a vaccine protects you from future illness. Success in one area of life often translates into success in other areas because of increased confidence in handling challenges.

What is Pragmatism?

It's a practical way of thinking, supported by philosophers like William James and John Dewey. **Instead of following strict rules or theories,**

pragmatism focuses on what actually works in real-life situations. We can use this approach in our daily lives to solve problems, make decisions, and deal with challenges.

Emotions can often cloud our judgment. So, having a clear and structured approach to problem-solving is quite necessary. Based on pragmatism, I am going to give you five steps you can use to solve any problem in your life. You can use it as a template for your problems and adjust it to your needs.

Step 1. Identify and Segment the Problem: Clearly define what the problem is. Don't look at symptoms only. We often tend to waste our time and energy on treating the symptoms rather than the root cause. So, understand the root cause of the problem. What is happening? When and where is it happening? Who is involved? Why is it a problem? Clearly defining the problem helps you avoid confusion and ensures that you're addressing the right issue.

For example, the biggest problem in your life could be that you're constantly feeling exhausted and overwhelmed at work. You might think the problem is simply "being too busy." But to solve it effectively, you need to segment the problem by asking simple questions to yourself.

What is happening?

You're feeling exhausted, overwhelmed, and unable to keep up with your tasks at work.

When and where is it happening?

This feeling starts mid-week and gets worse as the week progresses. It mainly occurs at your workplace, especially in the afternoons.

Who is involved?

You are the primary person affected, but it also impacts your coworkers because your productivity is decreasing.

Why is it a problem?

This exhaustion is affecting your performance at work, your mood, and even your personal life. You're not meeting deadlines, and the quality of your work is slipping, which could jeopardize your job security.

Instead of stopping at "I'm too busy," ask why. Is it because you have too many tasks? Are you working on tasks that could be delegated? Are you not managing your time well? Is there a lack of support from colleagues? Or are there underlying issues, such as poor sleep or health problems, contributing to your fatigue?

After reflecting, you realize that the root cause isn't just the workload. As you break the problem down into manageable segments, you realize that it's a combination of poor time management, taking on too many tasks without saying no, and not getting enough rest because of late nights. The problem isn't simply "being busy"; it's about how you're managing your time, boundaries, and self-care. Now you can focus on the right solutions, such as prioritizing tasks, delegating work, or setting better boundaries with your time. This prevents you from wasting time on surface-level solutions like working harder or longer hours, which won't address the root issue.

Step 2: Brainstorm possible solutions: In this step, jot down all possible solutions without judging them and without thinking whether they are perfect. Think creatively and consider all possibilities. If you can, involve other people in this and ask them for suggestions so that you can explore multiple approaches. Ask yourself what has worked before or what could be tried differently.

Let's continue with the above example of feeling exhausted at work and brainstorm some practical solutions to the problems we have broken down.

1. *Time Management Issues:*
   - Possible Solutions:
     - Create a daily to-do list and rank tasks by priority.
     - Use Google Calendar for time-blocking to schedule specific periods for focused work.
     - Set alarms or reminders to stay on track with high-priority tasks.
     - Delegate tasks to colleagues whenever possible.

- Experiment with the Pomodoro Technique (work for 25 minutes, then take a 5-minute break).

2. ***Difficulty Saying No:***
   - Possible Solutions:
     - Practice saying no whenever you can afford to say no.
     - Prepare polite but firm responses to decline additional work until the current work is finished.
     - Suggest alternatives when saying no, such as offering help at a later time or recommending someone else.
     - Set clear boundaries with colleagues about your workload capacity.
     - Use assertive communication training or workshops to improve your skills.

3. ***Lack of Rest and Self-Care:***
   - Possible Solutions:
     - Set a consistent bedtime and stick to it, even on weekends.
     - Schedule short breaks throughout the workday to stretch and relax.
     - Incorporate a short meditation or breathing exercise into your daily routine.
     - Stop wasting valuable time before sleep by limiting screen time before bed.

So, you see how there can be multiple solutions to one problem. Brainstorming like this helps you be more confident in your ability to solve the problem.

Step 3. Experiment with the solutions: Pragmatism values learning from experience. For each potential solution, consider the benefits and drawbacks. Also, consider the long-term impact of each solution, not just the immediate effects. Experiment with the solutions to find out what works best for you. For example, to-do lists might not be your thing, but you realize that Google Calendar helps you stay on track. Based on your evaluation, select the solution that best addresses the problem with the least negative consequences.

Pragmatism gives more importance to practical solutions over sticking to theoretical rules. If you find that working extra hours isn't helping you make progress, you shouldn't feel bound to continue with that approach just because it seems like the "hard work" route. Instead, focus on what actually helps you get things done effectively.

Step 4. Implement the Solution: After choosing the best solution, you need to implement it consistently for it to work well. Develop a step-by-step plan if necessary. You can also communicate the plan and delegate tasks to others involved in solving the problem if it's a collective problem.

Let's imagine that you have decided that practicing mindfulness and setting clearer boundaries between work and home is the best solution.

Implementation plan:

1. **Start Small:** You begin by dedicating 10 minutes every morning to mindfulness meditation. This helps you start the day with a clear and focused mind, reducing stress.

2. **Set Boundaries:** You decide on specific work hours and stick to them, turning off work notifications after a certain time in the evening to avoid burnout. This creates a clear separation between your work and personal life, allowing you to recharge.

3. **Communicate Your Plan:** You explain your new routine to your family and colleagues, so they understand and respect your boundaries. This step is crucial for getting their support and ensuring your plan works.

4. **Stay Consistent:** Even when you don't see immediate results, you continue with your mindfulness practice and boundary-setting. Over time, you start noticing a decrease in your stress levels and an increase in your overall well-being.

5. **Adjust as Needed:** As you implement your plan, you might realize that some things need to be changed. For example, you might find that evening mindfulness sessions are more effective for you, so you adjust your schedule accordingly.

Consistently implementing the solution gives it the time needed to take effect. Initial discomfort or slow progress doesn't mean the solution isn't working. Instead, it's part of the process of building patience which is an important element of emotional resilience.

Step 5. Monitor and Review:

Let's continue with the previous example where you've been implementing mindfulness and boundary-setting to manage stress and anxiety.

Monitoring the Results:

1. **Keep Track:** Start by journaling your stress levels and overall mood at the end of each day. Note down how well you stick to your work hours, how often you engage in mindfulness, and any changes in your stress or anxiety.

2. **Find Patterns:** Over a few weeks, you may begin to notice that your stress levels have decreased, and you feel more balanced. However, you may also observe that certain days are more stressful, particularly when unexpected work tasks spill into your personal time.

3. **Gather Feedback:** Ask your family and colleagues if they've noticed any changes in your behaviour or mood. Your family may mention that you seem less irritable, and your colleagues may appreciate that you're more focused during work hours.

4. **Evaluate the Impact:** You might realize that while your overall stress has decreased, the occasional spillover of work tasks still triggers anxiety. This indicates that while the solution is working, there's room for improvement.

Adjusting the Plan: Flexibility is key in a pragmatic approach. A new challenge like an unexpected workload could come up. Instead of sticking rigidly to your original plan, change your approach to fit the new situation.

5. **Make Adjustments:** To address the spillover issue, you decide to set even firmer boundaries by allocating time for handling unexpected tasks within your work hours. You also increase your mindfulness practice on particularly stressful days. You try to rest more and meditate for a longer duration during the weekends.

6. **Continuous Monitoring:** You continue to monitor your stress levels and make further adjustments as needed. Over time, you find a routine that consistently keeps your stress in check.

Once you have chosen and started implementing a solution, it doesn't mean that you are stuck with it even if it doesn't work as time goes on. You need to keep monitoring and reviewing to ensure that your solution is actually solving the problem. This will teach you one of the key elements of being resilient - being adaptable and open to change.

Resilience is about being practical and adaptable. It's not just about enduring tough times but about finding and using strategies that really work. So, we are going to add some practical exercises to our resilience toolbox in the next chapter.

Chapter - 20
Resilience-Building Toolbox

"Do not judge me by my success, judge me by how many times I fell down and got back up again."– **Nelson Mandela.**

In this chapter, we'll explore practical tools and strategies to help you cultivate resilience in your everyday life.

1. **Micro-Doses of Challenge:**

The concept is pretty simple. Instead of waiting for big, stressful situations to test your resilience, you proactively create little opportunities to push your comfort zone just a bit. Studies suggest that gradually exposing yourself to manageable stressors can enhance your resilience and improve your ability to cope with stress.

Going out of our comfort zone is intimidating for many of us. But expanding our comfort zone just a little sounds manageable. You can add small doses of challenge in your daily routine like striking up a conversation with a stranger, trying a new food, or taking a different route to work. Research by Sheldon Cohen highlights that these small, incremental challenges can help strengthen your stress response system and build resilience.

If you're a bit shy about meeting new people, start by setting a goal to make small talk with a colleague you haven't spoken to much. If you can't do that, just start by giving a smile. Sounds simple but even smiling at people is a brave act. Next, you might try introducing yourself to someone at a networking event or joining a new hobby group. Over time, these small, consistent challenges strengthen your ability to handle more significant social situations.

The beauty of this approach is that it doesn't require a dramatic change in your routine. Instead, it involves incorporating tiny, uncomfortable tasks into your daily routine. These micro-doses of challenge help you get used to expanding your comfort zone, making it easier to tackle larger challenges when they come your way.

2. Positive Stress Reframing

Research by Jamieson et al. found that when people look at stress as a positive force, it can enhance their ability to perform and reduce the negative effects of stress.

Stress as a positive force? How is that even possible? I thought so too. But imagine you're about to give an important presentation at work. Normally, the thought of standing in front of your colleagues would make you anxious and stressed. You might feel your heart racing, your palms sweating, and your thoughts becoming jumbled. Typically, you might see these signs as indicators that you're about to fail or mess up.

But what if you reframe your stress in a positive way? Instead of seeing your racing heart and nervous energy as a bad thing, you can think of it as your body getting ready to perform at its best—your brain is becoming more alert, and your body is gearing up to give you the energy you need to succeed. Stress can be a tool that helps you focus, think more clearly, and stay motivated. If a student is not stressed at all before an exam, he will not feel the need to focus on studying. The fact that you are stressed means that you care about your performance and that's a good thing. It makes you a responsible person. So, instead of letting the stress overwhelm you, you can use it to fuel your performance.

I hope you have heard of Elvis, the King of Rock 'n' Roll. He was pretty shy and introverted as a kid. He had a deep love for music and a natural talent for it, but he was often too nervous to perform in front of others. As his career took off, so did his nervousness. He was known to be extremely anxious before his performances. There are stories of Elvis waiting nervously backstage, pacing back and forth, before stepping out in front of thousands of fans. But once he was on stage, Elvis transformed. He channelled his nervous energy into his performances, captivating audiences with his unique style and magnetic stage presence.

What's incredibly impressive is that he didn't allow his weaknesses to hold him back; instead, he used them as stepping stones to reach greater heights.

I know it sounds kind of cliché when you come across a piece of advice that tells you to overcome your weaknesses. You must have heard it many times before. But this is one of those pieces of timeless wisdom that help you to live a good life. We often forget that our weaknesses do not define us and that we can always turn them into strengths.

The basic idea is to shift your perspective from seeing stress or nervousness as something that holds you back to something that is a positive force. Research shows that when people adopt this mindset, they're often able to perform better and experience fewer negative effects from stress. This is how you can use everything that stresses you out as an opportunity to build resilience.

Practical Exercises

1. The Challenge Ladder Worksheet

Exercise:
Create a "challenge ladder" by listing a series of tasks that gradually increase in difficulty. Start with the smallest challenge (e.g., saying hello to a colleague) and work your way up (e.g., giving a presentation at work). This exercise builds resilience by helping you take small, consistent steps toward bigger challenges.

Instructions:
- List 5 challenges, starting from the easiest task to the most difficult.
- Every day, tackle one challenge and note your progress.

Worksheet:

Step	Challenge	Completion Date	How did it feel?
1			
2			
3			

4			
5			

Source:

The concept of progressive challenge exposure comes from the work of Dr. Albert Bandura's self-efficacy theory (1977), which emphasizes building confidence through incremental success.

2. Elvis Mindset Shift Worksheet

Exercise:

Before a potentially stressful event (like a meeting, presentation, or important conversation), take five minutes to visualize the event going well. Imagine yourself using your nervous energy to stay focused and perform at your best. Think about how Elvis Presley transformed his nervousness into energy for his performances. Close your eyes and imagine yourself doing the same.

Instructions:

- Sit in a quiet space. Close your eyes and imagine yourself turning your nervousness into a positive outcome like Elvis did on stage.
- Picture the event unfolding positively. Imagine each detail: how you feel, how you speak, how others react.
- After the visualization, write down your thoughts and feelings before and after the exercise.

Worksheet:

- **Event Description (e.g., interview, speech):**

- **What are you nervous about?**

- **How can you turn that nervous energy into a positive force?**

_____

_____

- **How did this mindset shift help you approach the situation?**

_____

_____

Source:

This mindset shift is inspired by research on emotional reframing (Jamieson et al., 2012) and anecdotes from Elvis Presley's life, as documented in interviews and biographies.

Step - 5
RELEASE
Cultivate Self-Love And Forgiveness

This is the final step where you learn to release anything that holds you back from living the life you deserve. This step begins with learning to love yourself authentically. You will understand that self-care is not the same as self-love. You will also learn the gentle art of being kind to yourself. Finally, we will move on to the most challenging but essential step for healing: letting go of unconscious grudges and forgiving others and yourself.

Chapter - 21

Self-Care Can Soothe You; Self-Love Heals You

*"Owning our story and loving ourselves through that process is the bravest thing that we'll ever do." - **Brené Brown.***

These days, the concepts of self-care and self-love often get tossed around like they're the same thing. Self-care is a practice; self-love is a mindset. The actions you take to keep your mind, body, and soul in good shape are self-care. The reason why you do them is self-love. You can look at self-care as the maintenance work for your well-being. It's making sure you get enough sleep, eating your veggies, exercising, and taking time to relax and unwind.

Self-love means accepting yourself as you are, recognizing your worth, setting healthy boundaries, being your own biggest supporter, and making choices that honour your needs and values. It's the foundation of your relationship with yourself.

Self-Care	Self-Love
What you do for yourself	What you think about yourself
Taking a day off to rest	Not feeling guilty about resting.
Can be part of self-love	The foundation of your relationship with yourself
Can be influenced by external standards	Accepting yourself as you are, flaws and all
Your worth could depend on how you look/care for yourself	You are worthy no matter what

Self-care might be taking a day off to rest when you're exhausted; self-love is not feeling guilty about it. Self-care is eating a healthy meal; self-love is recognizing that you're worth nourishing, no matter your shape or size.

Self-care is more about doing, while self-love is about being. Self-care activities can be a part of self-love, but you can practice self-care without really loving yourself. You might go to the gym because you are influenced by body image standards on social media, not because you genuinely want to take care of your body.

Social media often blurs these lines and portrays self-care as the ultimate form of self-love. You see those Instagram posts with hashtags like #selfcare and #selflove showing someone in a bubble bath or on a beach vacation. While these activities can be part of both self-care and self-love, they don't capture the full picture. If someone cannot afford to vacation at exotic places and post such pictures, that doesn't mean they don't love themselves.

True self-love is an ongoing relationship with yourself, much deeper than an occasional pampering session.

Why Self-Love Is Essential for Your Well-being

Let's say you are on a journey, and you have a very negative backseat passenger. All they do throughout the journey is point out your mistakes and doubt your directions. Now imagine replacing that critic with a supportive friend who encourages you and believes in your ability as a good driver. Which one would make the trip more enjoyable?

That backseat passenger is your inner critic. Unfortunately, it's always with you, not just for one journey. The amount of self-love you have shaped your inner dialogue, and your inner dialogue shapes your reality. If you constantly tell yourself you're not good enough, you'll start to believe it. But if you start talking to yourself with love and respect, it will increase your self-worth and self-confidence. The way you talk to someone is very important in any relationship and the most important relationship is the one you have with yourself because it directly impacts the quality of your life. So, the way you talk to yourself is important because it decides what your relationship with yourself is going to be like – one that supports you or one that holds you back.

How you handle obstacles in life also depends on how much you love yourself. If you have a strong relationship with your spouse, you can face any hurdle together. Similarly, you can face any kind of downfall with resilience when you become your biggest supporter. You'll pick yourself up, dust yourself off, and continue your journey with renewed determination.

In the upcoming chapters we will learn how to cultivate a beautiful and loving relationship with the most important person in your life, YOU.

Chapter - 22

How To Love Yourself Truly, Deeply, And Madly

"How you love yourself is how you teach others to love you."
- Rupi Kaur.

Romantic movies and love stories sell us the notion that there is a perfect love waiting for you. You know, the kind where everything just clicks, and it feels like the universe has conspired to bring you and your soulmate together. We're told to believe that this kind of love is out there, somewhere, waiting to be found. But the truth is that the love you're seeking is already inside you.

Fairytale romances may have told you that you need to find someone who completes you to feel whole, cherished, and valued. But another person is not the only source of this magical love, and they can't be held responsible for completing you. You're already whole, not a piece of a puzzle. Another person can only add to your happiness and share theirs with you when you have already found it within you.

The longest relationship you will ever have is with yourself. So, self-love is the foundation of all other forms of love. How will another person know how to love you, when you don't know it yourself?

When you love yourself, you set the standard for how you deserve to be treated. You understand your worth and refuse to settle for less than you deserve. This inner love attracts the right kind of people and relationships into your life.

Let's see how we can learn to love ourselves truly, deeply, and madly. (Because you deserve nothing less.)

Accept your imperfections

Being human means having strengths and weaknesses. Accept all parts of yourself, including flaws and imperfections. However, many people confuse this with staying the same old version of themselves. Accepting yourself as you are doesn't mean that you will not make efforts to improve yourself in every way that you can. It only means that you learn to accept the things you can't change.

For example, you can't change your past actions. You can't change certain physical traits. But you can change your behaviour and habits. A smoker cannot say that he/she won't change because they love themselves and accept themselves for their weaknesses. If they truly love themselves, they will stop putting toxins in their body. Self-love is not an excuse for indulging in wrong habits and actions.

Date yourself

Get to know yourself on a deeper level by spending quality time alone doing things you enjoy. You can never finish knowing yourself. I didn't know I loved singing until I was thirty! Keep trying out new hobbies and new activities to discover more about yourself. Build a stronger, more intimate connection with yourself. A study by Harvard Business Review found that people who spend time alone are more likely to be creative and have a better understanding of themselves. So, reflect on your interests, passions, and dreams no matter how old you are. You might discover hidden talents and interests that could also become career opportunities and propel your life in a new direction.

Practice Unconditional Self-Compassion

Treat yourself with the same kindness, support, and understanding that you'd offer a best friend. When you make a mistake or face challenges, comfort yourself and silence the inner critic. Let go of past mistakes and practice self-forgiveness. I know it's not easy. We tend to beat ourselves up for our mistakes. But understand that everyone makes errors, and it's a part of learning and growing. We'll learn more about this in the next chapter.

Be Careful of the Inner Dialogue

When negative thoughts arise, question their validity. Replace them with positive affirmations and truths about your worth and capabilities. Create a list of positive affirmations about yourself and repeat them daily. You can use the techniques given in Step 3 for this. Rule of thumb: If you wouldn't say it to someone you love, don't say it to yourself.

Take Care of Your Body, Mind, and Soul

Pay attention to your body's signals and emotional needs. If you're tired, rest. If you're stressed, find ways to relax. Taking care of yourself is a fundamental aspect of deep self-love. This includes proper nutrition, exercise, relaxation, and hobbies that bring you joy.

Without self-love, we cannot fully become our best selves. Being your best version means letting go of your weaknesses and the things that drag you down. You likely know what isn't good for you, yet you may still cling to those habits because they are familiar. So, knowing what's right for you is not enough.

Very often, we do not change our habits because we are afraid that we will fail and put ourselves down. But when there is room for compassion, when you allow yourself to fail, you can try new things without the fear of being judged or labelled as a failure by your own mind. And believe me, being viewed as a failure by others is far less damaging than feeling like a failure in your own eyes.

Protect Your Energy

Protect your energy and well-being by setting healthy boundaries with others. Respecting your limits is essential for deep self-love. You may find this difficult if you're a people pleaser. It's hard to disappoint people but if you don't, you risk disappointing yourself.

You can't continuously give your energy to those who take it for granted without reciprocating. Healthy relationships require a two-way exchange of positivity. If you're not receiving that from others, it may be time to reassess those connections.

Welcome tough conversations and speak up for yourself

I used to think that to keep things peaceful in all my relationships, I should avoid tough talks. Why invite trouble, right? But instead of making things better, it made them worse. The problems didn't disappear, they just got bigger and messier. If I had just spoken up about what bothered me from the beginning, I could have saved those friendships.

Choosing to avoid difficult conversations might seem like the path of least resistance, but it often leads to resentment and misunderstandings. When you don't speak up for yourself and convey what hurt you, you're essentially letting the other person treat you the same way in the future.

Standing up for yourself is the ultimate act of self-love. Don't worry about the outcome. If you end up parting ways with a friend after a tough talk, it just means you've saved yourself from a friendship that wasn't genuine. A friendship where you can't talk about what bothers you isn't really a friendship, right?

Keeping up friendships takes time and energy, both of which are limited. So, you've got a choice to make. Would you rather have a few real friends or a bunch of fake ones?

Celebrate Yourself

A study from the University of California found that celebrating small wins can boost motivation and overall happiness. We tend to downplay our achievements because we think they don't matter. (Remember cognitive distortion: Minimization) You need to do the opposite. Even if you achieved something very small, appreciate and treat yourself to something special. It will increase your self-worth and make you even more motivated. Try keeping a "wins" journal where you note down your achievements, no matter how small, and reward yourself regularly.

Always keep learning

Albert Einstein said, *"Once you stop learning, you start dying."* Do activities that challenge and expand your skills and knowledge like taking online courses or reading books on topics you're curious about. Set aside an hour a day to learn whatever you wish. Be addicted to learning. The more you focus on personal growth, the more your confidence and self-love grow. You become a magnet for new opportunities. Lifelong learning not only sharpens your mind but also opens doors to new adventures and possibilities.

Respect others

Some people confuse self-love with self-obsession and put themselves on a pedestal while ignoring everyone else. That's not self-love. True self-love doesn't just mean treating yourself with kindness and respect, it also involves recognizing and respecting the worth and needs of others.

The way you treat others is the way you treat yourself. The way I have come to understand self-love is that it is the reflection of your inner health. Just like our physical health is evident through how we look, how much you love yourself can be seen in how you interact with other people. Self-love leads to self-respect which shows in everything you do, the friends you choose, the habits you nurture, and the personal goals you set.

It's simple: Treat yourself well, while not harming others. Treat others well, while not harming yourself.

- Mark Manson

If you are curious to know what can happen for you if you really start loving yourself, here's a brief list of things that will unfold.

1. **Self-acceptance**
2. **Inner peace**
3. **Emotional resilience**
4. **Improved relationships**
5. **Setting and respecting boundaries**
6. **Personal growth and development**
7. **Increased confidence and self-esteem**
8. **Better decision-making**
9. **Enhanced physical and mental well-being**
10. **Greater compassion and empathy towards yourself and others**

11. **Fulfilment and happiness**
12. **Authenticity and living in alignment with your values**
13. **Courage to pursue dreams and goals**
14. **Reduced stress and anxiety**
15. **Gratitude and appreciation for life's blessings.**

Learning to love yourself is the magic ingredient when it comes to achieving your goals and desires. It's not that surprising when you understand it deeply. One of the first outcomes of loving yourself unconditionally is an increase in your own worthiness. When you believe that you are worth something, and you deserve it, you can then find the courage to take action. Self-love helps you to overcome limiting beliefs that are often the result of fear or past experiences. When you no longer criticize yourself for something you did in the past, you are no longer chained to it which allows you to create a new reality.

Practical exercise:

Self-Love Letter Exercise:

Instructions

1. *Acknowledge Your Strengths and Achievements:*
   - Reflect on your strengths, achievements, and qualities that you are proud of. For example:
     - "I am proud of how you handled [specific situation]."
     - "I appreciate your ability to [strength/skill]."
     - "I am grateful for your [achievement or personal trait]."

2. *Express Compassion for Your Challenges:*
   - Recognize and offer compassion to yourself for any challenges or difficulties you have faced. For example:
     - "I understand that you have struggled with [challenge], and that's okay."

- "I forgive you for [past mistake], and I know that you are growing and learning."

Reflection

1. **Read Your Letter**: After writing your letter, read it through and reflect on the feelings it evokes. Notice how it impacts your mood and self-perception.

2. **Keep the Letter Accessible:** Store your letter in a place where you can revisit it whenever you need a boost of self-love and affirmation.

3. **Practice Regularly:** Make this self-love letter exercise a regular practice.

Here is an example letter for you:

Dear (insert name),

I'm taking a moment to write this letter to you, to remind you of how truly amazing and deserving you are.

I want to start by celebrating your strengths and achievements. I am proud of how you managed [specific situation], showing remarkable strength. Your ability to [strength/skill] is something that not only impresses others but also brings you closer to your goals. Remember how you accomplished [achievement] despite the challenges? That was no small feat.

I know the past year has been difficult for you but it's okay to struggle with [challenge]—it doesn't define you or diminish your worth. I forgive you for [past mistake], and I recognize the courage it took to face and learn from it. You have grown so much from these experiences, and I admire your strength and perseverance.

What makes you truly unique is your [unique quality]. Your [positive trait] brings so much positivity and warmth to those around you. Whether it's your [specific action or behaviour] or your ability to [another unique quality], you make a difference in the lives of others, and that is something to be celebrated.

You are deserving of love and care, and you have the strength to overcome any obstacles that come your way. I trust in your ability to handle whatever challenges arise and to continue growing into the amazing person you are meant to be.

With love and kindness,

[Your Name]

Chapter - 23
Self-Compassion: The Gentle Art Of Being kind To Yourself

*"You have been criticizing yourself for years, and it hasn't worked. Try approving of yourself and see what happens." -**Louise L. Hay.***

It's easy to love ourselves when things are going well but it's not that easy when we fail or make mistakes. That's where self-compassion comes into play. Self-compassion means recognizing that suffering, failure, and making mistakes are part of the shared human experience, and instead of harshly judging ourselves, we offer ourselves the kindness and care we deserve.

You might feel that if you love yourself, you will naturally be compassionate toward yourself. But it's not always true. While self-love is about valuing yourself, self-compassion is about how you treat yourself when things go wrong. Do you treat yourself with kindness or do you beat yourself up? Self-compassion involves being gentle, understanding, and non-judgmental towards yourself, especially when you experience pain or setbacks. Instead of criticizing or punishing yourself for not meeting certain standards, self-compassion tells you to look at your struggles with kindness. When you can be kind to yourself, even in the face of your failures, you open the door to healing and growth.

How to develop self-compassion
Self-compassion is essential for emotional healing. Kristin Neff, a leading researcher on self-compassion, explains that developing self-compassion involves three key components: self-kindness, common humanity, and mindfulness. Neff describes self-kindness as being warm and understanding towards ourselves, especially when we fail or feel

inadequate. This means acknowledging that everyone makes mistakes and not letting our painful thoughts consume us.

1. *Self-Kindness vs. Self-Judgment*

Self-kindness means being warm and understanding towards yourself, especially when you experience pain, failure, or feelings of inadequacy. Instead of ignoring your suffering or criticizing yourself harshly, treat yourself with gentleness and care.

Imagine you're trying to learn a new skill, like cooking a challenging recipe. After several attempts, the dish still doesn't turn out right. Instead of thinking, "I'm hopeless in the kitchen" or "I'll never get this," practice self-kindness. Tell yourself, "It's okay to struggle. Learning takes time, and each attempt is part of the process."

Think about how you would support a friend facing the same situation. Would you tell them they're a failure? Probably not! You'd likely say, "You're doing great for trying something new! Keep going; you'll get it next time!"

2. *Common Humanity vs. Isolation*

Common humanity involves recognizing that everyone goes through tough times, and feeling inadequate is something all people experience. This perspective helps you understand that you're not alone in your struggles, which can be incredibly comforting.

Let's say you're going through a breakup. It's easy to feel like you're the only one experiencing this kind of pain, leading to feelings of isolation and loneliness. However, reminding yourself that breakups are a common human experience can be helpful.

Think about the countless songs, movies, and books about heartbreak. They exist because so many people go through similar situations. The fact that many have gone through it also means many have found the way to healing.

You might talk to friends who have gone through breakups and realize that your feelings are shared by many, helping you feel less alone.

Some communities bring together individuals who share similar experiences, such as battling illness or navigating personal loss. When people are going through something as challenging as a cancer diagnosis, it's easy for them to feel isolated. In these groups, whether online or in-person, people find a space where they can openly share their fears, frustrations, and hopes with others who *truly* understand what they're going through. It reminds participants that they are not alone and that their struggles are part of a larger human experience.

3. Mindfulness vs. Over-Identification

Mindfulness is about accepting your painful thoughts and feelings, rather than letting them consume you. It can prevent you from over-identifying with your pain.

Suppose you're feeling anxious about an upcoming exam. Being mindful means accepting your anxiety without letting it take over your entire mental space. Instead of thinking, "I'm going to fail; I can't handle this," practice mindfulness by observing your thoughts and feelings without judgment. You might say to yourself, "I'm feeling anxious right now, and that's okay. I've prepared as best as I can." Try techniques like deep breathing or meditation to help centre yourself and keep your anxiety in check.

The Science Behind Self-Compassion

Self-compassion might seem like a simple concept—being kind to yourself when things go wrong—but it has deep roots in psychological research, and its benefits are far-reaching.

1. **The Role of the Brain:** When we face failure or criticism, our brain's default response is often to activate the threat defence system. This is the same system that would trigger our fight-or-flight response in dangerous situations. When we're harsh on ourselves, our brain interprets it as a threat, leading to stress, anxiety, and a cascade of negative emotions.

   However, practicing self-compassion can shift this response. Research shows that self-compassion activates the parasympathetic nervous system, which is responsible for calming the body and reducing stress. It also triggers the release of oxytocin, often referred to as the "love hormone." Oxytocin helps us feel safe, connected, and cared for, counteracting the stress response.

2. **Psychological Resilience:** Studies by Dr. Kristin Neff, a pioneer in self-compassion research, have shown that people who practice self-compassion are more resilient in the face of challenges. Instead of spiralling into self-criticism, they are better able recover from setbacks. This is because self-compassion helps create a shield against negative emotions, allowing you to cope more effectively with difficult situations.

3. **Reducing the Impact of Negative Bias:** Our brain is naturally wired to focus more on negative experiences than positive ones, a phenomenon known as Negativity Bias. This bias can lead to overthinking, depression and anxiety. Self-compassion acts as an antidote to this bias. By consciously treating ourselves with kindness and understanding, we can reduce the impact of negative thoughts and prevent them from taking over our emotions.

4. **Enhancing Emotional Intelligence:** Self-compassion also enhances emotional intelligence because when we practice self-compassion, we become more attuned to our emotions. It allows us to respond to our feelings in a balanced way, rather than reacting impulsively or suppressing them. Over time, this makes you a more stable and positive person.

5. **Long-Term Mental Health Benefits:** Research has also shown that self-compassion is linked to lower levels of anxiety and depression and higher levels of life satisfaction and overall well-being. Self-esteem can fluctuate based on external achievements or comparisons, but self-compassion provides a stable source of self-worth that isn't dependent on external factors.

Practical Exercise:

1. Self-Compassion Break by Dr. Kristin Neff

Purpose: To create an immediate shift towards self-compassion during moments of distress.

How to Practice:

1. Identify the Feeling: When you notice a moment of self-criticism or emotional struggle, pause and acknowledge the feeling.
2. Remind Yourself: Say to yourself, "This is a moment of suffering. Suffering is part of being human."
3. Offer Kindness: Speak gently to yourself, using phrases like, "I'm here for you," or "It's okay to feel this way."
4. Reflect: Spend a few moments reflecting on the feeling and your response. Notice any changes in your emotional state.

Benefits: This exercise helps you quickly shift from self-criticism to self-compassion.

2. Compassionate Body Scan

This is a mindfulness practice that focuses on becoming aware of physical sensations in your body and responding with kindness and care.

How to Practice:

- Lie down in a comfortable position and close your eyes.
- Starting from your toes, move slowly upward, paying attention to any tension or discomfort in your body.
- As you become aware of discomfort, imagine sending kindness and warmth to those areas.
- Continue scanning your body, allowing relaxation to flow through.

    Source: *Kabat-Zinn, Jon. Full Catastrophe Living: Using the Wisdom of Your Body and Mind to Face Stress, Pain, and Illness.*

Chapter - 24

Is It Possible To Carry A Grudge And Not Be Aware Of It?

"Pain and suffering are a kind of currency passed from hand to hand until they reach someone who receives them but does not pass them on."

-Simon Weil.

Your brain can sneakily hold onto unresolved anger, resentment, or hurt, pushing these feelings deep in the subconscious. We like to think that we can just lock away memories and emotions we want to forget. We want to protect ourselves from feeling the pain again. So, when you get hurt or betrayed, your brain sometimes decides to shove those negative feelings into the back room, out of sight. It can make you think that you have moved on and you don't have anything against anyone. But just because the grudges are hidden doesn't mean they're gone—they're just simmering away, waiting to make an unexpected outburst.

The Science Behind Unconscious Grudges

We already know that our brain's limbic system, especially the amygdala, is like the emotional command centre. It handles how we feel and remember things. When we experience emotional pain, the amygdala attaches strong feelings to those memories. If the feelings are too intense, our brain might try to hide them to protect us from immediate distress. But those hidden emotions don't go away and can influence our behaviour and feelings in ways we don't realize.

Consider this common scenario: You had a falling out with a friend years ago. It hurt so much that your mind decided to tuck that pain away. Fast forward to today, and you find yourself snapping at people or feeling unusually anxious without really knowing why. That's your brain's way of saying, "Hey, remember that unresolved stuff? It's still here!"

Research backs this up. Unresolved emotional issues, like grudges, can increase your stress and anxiety levels. When the stress becomes chronic, it can affect your health causing high blood pressure, a weakened immune system, digestive issues, and even skin problems. It's like carrying around a backpack full of rocks everywhere you go.

So, what should you do? You need to bring these hidden grudges into the light even if it's going to be uncomfortable. It's necessary for your emotional healing and overall health. You need to dig out these buried feelings so that you can start to lighten your emotional load and improve your well-being. Let's learn how to spot these unconscious grudges.

Signs of Unconscious Grudges:
- Feeling irritated for no reason, snapping at people for minor disagreements
- Avoiding certain people or places without really knowing why
- Stress-related headaches or muscle tension
- Struggling to trust people
- Persistent negative thoughts about yourself or others

Alright, so maybe now you've started to recognize if you're holding a grudge, or maybe you've always known you're hurt by someone and believe it's impossible to forgive them. I get it. It's tough. And I'm not here to tell you to just let go of those feelings or your anger. Seeking revenge feels way more satisfying, doesn't it? It's like an adrenaline rush.

Also, forgiving someone might seem like you're inviting more bad behaviour from them or others in the future. You may want to set an example that people just cannot do this to you. They deserve to pay for what they did, right? But here's a thought you might like to consider: while they may not deserve to be forgiven, do you deserve the peace that comes with forgiving them?

When you decide not to forgive someone, you choose to carry the weight of anger and resentment every day; it can be exhausting. It spills over into every aspect of your life, affecting your relationships, your work, and your happiness.

> *Forgiving someone doesn't change their actions or decrease the impact of what they did, but it does give you peace of mind. Do you deserve to be weighed down by resentment, or do you deserve the freedom and peace that forgiveness can bring?*

The choice to forgive or not is yours but you should be aware of the consequences of each choice and then you can make an informed decision. As Ankur Wari Koo says, *decisions in life should be made from a point of awareness, not ignorance.*

Choice #1 I will not forgive.

Let's say you decided not to forgive someone. Here are some possibilities to consider:

Mental health problems: It can escalate conflicts and perpetuate a cycle of hurt and retaliation. Imagine walking with ankle weights. Negative emotions of anger and resentment can weigh heavily on your heart. It's not just the feelings that are affected. This emotional baggage can cloud your judgment, influence your interactions, and drain your energy. You won't be able to focus on the positive aspects of life. You may feel like you can choose not to forgive someone and still enjoy your life. But to truly enjoy your life, you need to be grateful for your life. Feeling grateful for your life and holding onto the thought that someone wronged you are two things that simply cannot coexist. It will create chronic stress and lead to mental health issues like anxiety and depression.

Strained Relationships: The anger and mistrust you feel towards one person can create a barrier to forming healthy, trusting relationships with others. It's not fair, right? When you choose not to heal yourself, some of that anger will inevitably spill over into your other relationships.

Physical Health Issues: Your body makes note of everything you think. The stress and emotional turmoil from holding onto a grudge can manifest physically. It can lead to a host of health problems, including high blood pressure, a weakened immune system, and an increased risk of heart disease.

Stagnation in Personal Growth: When you go through any challenge, you are meant to learn from it and grow but refusing to forgive can put a brake on your personal development. Because forgiveness is often a key part of healing and moving forward, and without it, your personal growth can be stunted.

Limited Joy and Fulfilment: You may find it difficult to fully enjoy life's positive experiences if you are constantly burdened by unresolved anger. If you cannot forget the hurtful experiences, they can trigger negative emotions and stress responses. I know you can't make yourself forget things. But you can certainly stop being obsessed with the memories.

Sometimes we get used to the pain and without it, we don't know who we are. The pain becomes our identity. But if you constantly remind yourself of the hurt, it can prevent you from fully moving on and finding peace.

Why revisit the pain? It will just keep the wound open, making it harder to let go of negative emotions and truly heal. Pain is not your identity. It is only a teacher who is here to teach you for a certain period of time, and you are meant to learn the lesson and move on to the next class.

Reduced Empathy and Compassion: You might have come across people who shut the doors to everyone after a betrayal or a fallout with somebody. Unforgiveness can harden your heart, making it more difficult to empathize with others and show compassion. It just keeps you emotionally tied to the person who hurt you. Do you really want them to have that kind of power over you?

Choice #2: I am ready to forgive.

Forgiving doesn't mean they did right or that you are weak. It just means that you have chosen to free yourself from the control the past has over you. Here's what can happen for you if you decide to forgive someone completely:

Your mental health will improve:

A study published in the Journal of Consulting and Clinical Psychology found that people who practiced forgiveness experienced lower levels of stress and anxiety. The act of forgiveness activated areas of the brain associated with empathy and emotional regulation, suggesting that forgiveness can shift our emotional state from one of distress to one of calm and control.

Your heart will thank you:

Forgiveness is good for your heart! The Annals of Behavioural Medicine published a study showing that those who forgive others easily had lower blood pressure and a healthier heart. Holding onto anger and resentment can literally make you sick, while forgiveness promotes physical health.

Your relationships will flourish:

Forgiveness also plays an important role in the quality of our relationships. When we forgive, we can make room for positivity and rebuild trust and intimacy with others. Couples who practiced forgiveness reported feeling closer and more committed to each other. Another study published in the journal *Personal Relationships* showed that forgiveness is associated with higher relationship satisfaction and stability.

You will experience growth:

Holding onto grudges can keep you so preoccupied that you don't have time to focus on learning new things and improving your life. Forgiving someone is no easy feat, but when you achieve it, your self-respect increases, and you gain a better understanding of others. This growth mindset can help you turn painful experiences into valuable lessons.

If you don't want to forgive someone, that's fine too. Don't force yourself to forgive. There is a third choice.

Choice #3 I can learn from the experience and grow.

I understand that sometimes you may not completely forget what happened and forgive the person. In such situations, allow yourself to grieve and process the lessons. When someone wrongs you, there is a lesson you need to learn. But most people are pressured to forgive others even before they have fully processed the impact of what was done to them. Forgiveness comes with a lot of benefits but forcing yourself to forgive will negate those benefits and can make you resent yourself.

So, the third choice is that you use the experience as a lesson for personal growth and wisdom until you are ready to fully let it go. In some situations, it's important to give yourself time to internalize the lessons before moving on. You will keep falling into the same pit if you don't remember its location. This choice allows you to let go of resentment while still retaining the valuable insights gained from the situation, helping you to move forward with a deeper understanding.

It's possible to remember what happened in a way that doesn't hold onto pain but instead uses the memory as a guide for wiser future actions. This gives you time to work on healing the emotional impact of the event.

Remember, every situation doesn't require the same response. In some cases, it might be healthier to forget and fully move on, while in others, remembering is important for your safety and growth.

The Challenge of Forgiving Yourself

Forgiving yourself can be even harder than forgiving others because it involves facing your inner critic. This inner critic magnifies your mistakes and keeps reminding you of your guilt and shame. You can distance yourself from others who criticize you, but your inner critic is always present, making it difficult to escape its harsh judgment.

Many of us hold ourselves to incredibly high standards. When we fall short, we blame ourselves. If you have a perfectionist mindset it leaves little room for compassion or understanding when you make mistakes.

Think about it: there are things you do and things you don't do based on your internal sense of what's right and wrong. When you do something that goes against this sense, it can shatter your self-image, which is the foundation of your identity. When this foundation is broken, forgiving yourself can feel impossible.

Guilt and shame are powerful emotions that come with making mistakes. While guilt can motivate us to make amends, too much guilt or shame can be paralyzing. Shame, in particular, makes us feel deeply flawed and unworthy, making it hard to move past our errors and love ourselves.

Another reason self-forgiveness is tough is the fear of repeating past mistakes. We might think that holding onto guilt will prevent us from making the same errors again. However, it just traps us in a cycle of self-punishment rather than making room for real growth.

> *If you are a human, it's impossible to not have any regrets. We dream about reaching our deathbed without any regrets but it's just a wishful fantasy.*

As Kathryn Schulz says, "The point is not living without regrets, the point is to not hate ourselves for having them. We need to learn to love the flawed imperfect things we create and to forgive ourselves for creating them. Regret need not remind us that we did badly. It reminds us that we can do better."

Beautiful thought, right? Even regret can teach you so many things. You regret something only when you go against your own values. So, it reminds you of your values and tells you to stick to them to live a peaceful life in the future. Once you have learned all that you can from your experience, the wisest thing to do is forgive yourself and move on.

If you have decided to forgive and let go, you might be wondering, "I'm ready to forgive, but how exactly do I do it?" Deciding to let go is the first and most difficult step and I want to congratulate you for making that decision. It takes a heart of gold to forgive someone or yourself. There are many ways to go about this. The most effective method that has worked for me and many others is ACT – Acceptance and Commitment Therapy.

Acceptance and Commitment Therapy (ACT) is a powerful psychological intervention that combines mindfulness skills with values-based living. Let's learn how we can use it for forgiveness.

ACT is based on six core principles:

1. **Cognitive Defusion:** This is about seeing your thoughts for what they are—just thoughts—not letting them dominate your mind. When your mind says, "I'm not good enough." Instead of believing it completely, look at it like a passing cloud of thought. If you're holding a grudge because someone wronged you, instead of letting that thought take over, you acknowledge it and see it as a part of your mind's chatter.

2. **Acceptance:** Allowing yourself to feel your emotions fully without trying to change or avoid them. Instead of fighting against your feelings, you allow them to be. So, if you're angry at someone, instead of telling yourself, "I shouldn't feel this way," you accept that, yes, you do feel this way. It's okay to feel hurt.

3. **Contact with the Present Moment:** Being fully aware and engaged with your current experience, rather than being lost in thoughts about the past or future. Grudges keep you stuck in the past. ACT encourages you to focus on the now. Mindfulness practices, like paying attention to your breath or noticing the world around you, bring you back to the present.

4. **Observing Self:** Recognizing that you are not your thoughts, feelings, or memories. You're the observer of these thoughts and feelings, not just a person full of grudges. This perspective helps create a bit of distance from the negativity.

5. **Values:** Identifying what is truly important to you and what you want your life to stand for. For example, you value peace or kindness. By focusing on these values, you start to see how holding onto grudges doesn't serve you. Instead, you practice kindness and forgive the person who wronged you.

6. **Committed Action:** Once you know what your values are, take steps no matter how small, towards living a life that reflects your values. If forgiveness aligns with your value of peace, then you start taking steps towards forgiving, even if it's just a little bit at a time.

Let's say you've been holding a grudge against a friend who betrayed your trust. Using ACT, you might start by acknowledging the pain and anger you feel without judgment (Acceptance).

Then, you see these feelings as just a part of your experience, not the whole of you (Observing Self).

You focus on the present moment, perhaps through mindfulness exercises like deep breathing (Contact with the Present Moment).

By identifying your value of maintaining peace, you realize that letting go of this grudge aligns with your values (Values).

Finally, you take small steps towards forgiveness, like writing a letter (you don't have to send it!) expressing your feelings and desire to move on (Committed Action).

Practical Exercise: Forgiveness letter

This exercise helps you release lingering resentment or guilt by writing a forgiveness letter, whether to someone else or yourself.

Step 1: Identify the Recipient
- Reflect on a person or situation that has caused you pain or a mistake you've made that you struggle to forgive.

Step 2: Write About the Hurt
- Briefly describe what happened and how it made you feel.

Example: "You hurt me when you... It made me feel..."

Step 3: Acknowledge Your Emotions
- Recognize your feelings as valid. Express how the situation affected you, but also acknowledge your desire to move on.

Step 4: Express Forgiveness
- State your intention to forgive. This isn't about excusing the behaviour but choosing to release the negative emotions tied to it.

Example: "I forgive you for... I choose to let go of this pain."

Step 5: Let Go
- Conclude the letter with a statement of release, affirming your commitment to moving forward.

Example: "I am letting go of this hurt and choosing peace."

Final Step: Symbolic Release

- After writing the letter, you may choose to keep it, tear it up, or safely burn it—whatever feels right to you—as a symbolic act of letting go.

This exercise is a simple yet powerful way to free yourself from emotional burdens and move toward a more peaceful, resilient self.

Example Letter

Dear [Name],

I want to take this moment to express my feelings regarding what happened between us. When you [describe the event], it made me feel deeply hurt and betrayed. This incident has affected me in many ways and caused emotional pain.

I understand that everyone makes mistakes, and I've tried to see things from your perspective. Maybe you acted out of fear, confusion, or stress. Whatever the reasons, I recognize that we are all human and imperfect.

Today, I choose to forgive you for [specific action]. I no longer want to carry the burden of anger and resentment. I want to let go of this pain and find peace.

I hope that we can both heal and move forward from this experience. I wish you well and hope that we can both grow from what has happened.

Wishing you peace,

[Your Name]

Begin Your Reset

As you reach the end of this book, remember that the journey of your emotional reset is just beginning. You are now armed with the fundamental knowledge needed to transform your life. Knowledge is great but useless without action. So, I urge you to complete the practical exercises in this book. Don't wait for the perfect moment, because that moment is now.

If you need guidance or support, don't hesitate to reach out. You can connect with me directly through my Instagram page **@drketakip** and share what you learned from this book. Tag me so we can celebrate your wins together!

Sharing your experiences can be powerful, not just for you, but for others who may be on a similar journey. I'd love to hear about your progress. So, please leave a review on Amazon or the website where you purchased this book from.

Thank you for allowing me to be a part of your journey. Remember, you have the power to reset, heal, and grow. Let's continue this journey together.

About The Author

Hi, I'm Dr. Ketaki Pawar Chavan—a mom, entrepreneur, blogger, YouTuber, author, speaker, certified CBT life coach, and Oral and Maxillofacial Surgeon with a passion for continuous learning.

I love spending time understanding how we can transform our lives by shifting our thought patterns. I believe that gaining control over the mind is the key to unlocking massive transformation in life. It's incredible how things start to change when you learn to recognize and reframe negative thoughts.

When I'm not working, writing, or shooting videos, you'll find me reading, singing, exercising, meditating, cooking, or enjoying time with my daughter and husband.

You can connect with me here:

My Blog: https://medium.com/@drketaki.oms

YouTube Channel: https://www.youtube.com/@TheLifeStartup

My Instagram: @drketakip

Email: drketaki.oms@gmail.com

LinkedIn:https://www.linkedin.com/in/dr-ketaki-pawar-chavan-4879a7152/

Bibliography

1. Negativity Bias: Vaish A, Grossmann T, Woodward A. Not all emotions are created equal: the negativity bias in social-emotional development. Psychol Bull. 2008;134(3):383-403. doi:10.1037/0033-2909.134.3.383

2. Hansenne M. Valuing Happiness is Not a Good Way of Pursuing Happiness, but Prioritizing Positivity is A Replication Study. Psychol Belg. 2021;61(1):306-314. Published 2021 Nov 10. doi:10.5334/pb.1036

3. The happiness paradox: Felicia K Zerwas, Brett Q Ford, The paradox of pursuing happiness, Current Opinion in Behavioural Sciences, Volume 39, 2021, Pages 106-112, ISSN 2352-1546, https://doi.org/10.1016/j.cobeha.2021.03.006.

4. Schooler JW, Mauss IB. To be happy and to know it: The experience and meta-awareness of pleasure. In: Kringelbach ML, Berridge KC, editors. Pleasures of the Brain. New York, NY: Oxford University Press; 2010. pp. 244–254.

5. Catalino LI, Algoe SB, Fredrickson BL. Prioritizing positivity: an effective approach to pursuing happiness? [published correction appears in Emotion. 2015 Apr;15(2):175. doi: 10.1037/emo0000064] [published correction appears in Emotion. 2016 Apr;16(3):319. doi: 10.1037/emo0000177]. Emotion.2014;14(6):1155-1161.doi:10.1037/a0038029

6. Happiness set point theory: Lyubomirsky S, Sheldon KM, Schkade D. Pursuing happiness: The architecture of sustainable change. Review of General Psychology. 2005;9(2):111-1311.

7. Letting Go Ritual: This exercise is influenced by mindfulness and acceptance-based practices found in therapies like Acceptance and Commitment Therapy (ACT) and Dialectical Behaviour Therapy (DBT). These therapies often incorporate rituals or symbolic acts as a way of helping individuals let go of unhelpful thoughts and emotions. The idea of

releasing thoughts or pressures by writing them down and then symbolically destroying or releasing the paper is a common therapeutic technique.

8. Enough List: This concept is rooted in the philosophy of sufficiency and gratitude. It is often seen in positive psychology practices that encourage individuals to recognize and appreciate what they already have, rather than constantly striving for more. This practice can also be linked to Cognitive Behavioural Therapy (CBT), where shifting from scarcity thinking to an appreciation of sufficiency helps reduce anxiety and dissatisfaction.

9. Savoring Practice: Savoring is a well-documented concept in positive psychology. It was extensively discussed by Fred B. Bryant and Joseph Veroff in their book "Savoring: A New Model of Positive Experience". Savoring involves fully experiencing and enjoying the positive aspects of life, and it has been shown to enhance well-being and increase happiness. This practice encourages mindfulness and the intentional focus on positive experiences as they occur.

10. Post-traumatic growth: Tedeschi RG, Calhoun LG. Posttraumatic Growth: Conceptual Foundations and Empirical Evidence. Psychological Inquiry. 2004;15(1):1-18

11.Evolutionary Roots: Baumeister RF, Bratslavsky E, Finkenauer C, Vohs KD. Bad is stronger than good. Rev Gen Psychol. 2001;5(4):323-370. doi:10.1037/1089-2680.5.4.323.

12. Early Life Experiences: Anda RF, Felitti VJ, Bremner JD, et al. The enduring effects of abuse and related adverse experiences in childhood. Eur Arch Psychiatry Clin Neurosci. 2006;256(3):174-186. doi:10.1007/s00406-005-0624-4.

13. Learned Behaviour: Bandura A. Social Learning Theory. Englewood Cliffs, NJ: Prentice Hall; 1977.

14. Media and Environment: Nabi RL, Myrick JG. Uplifting fear appeals: Considering the role of hope in fear-based persuasive messages. Health Commun. 2019;34(4):463-474. doi:10.1080/10410236.2017.1422847.

15. Fardouly J, Diedrichs PC, Vartanian LR, Halliwell E. Social comparisons on social media: the impact of Facebook on young women's

body image concerns and mood. Body Image. 2015;13:38-45. doi:10.1016/j.bodyim.2014.12.002

16. Journaling has been shown to improve mental health by promoting self-awareness and emotional regulation (Pennebaker JW, Chung CK. Expressive writing: Connections to physical and mental health. In Friedman HS, ed. Encyclopedia of Mental Health. 2nd ed. Academic Press; 2016:202-212).

17. Kobau, R, Sniezek, J, Zack, M M, Lucas, RE, Burns, A. Well-Being Assessment: An Evaluation of Well-Being Scales for Public Health and Population Estimates of Well-Being among US Adults. Applied Psychology: 2010: 2: 272-297. doi.org/10.1111/j.1758-0854.2010.01035.x

18. Maier, S. F., & Seligman, M. E. (1976). Learned helplessness: Theory and evidence. Journal of Experimental Psychology: General, 105(1), 3–46. doi:10.1037/0096-3445.105.1.3

19. Allison PJ, Guichard C, Gilain L. A prospective investigation of dispositional optimism as a predictor of health-related quality of life in head and neck cancer patients. Qual Life Res. 2000;9(8):951-960. doi:10.1023/a:1008931906253

20. Radcliffe, Nathan & Klein, William. (2002). Dispositional, Unrealistic, and Comparative Optimism: Differential Relations with the Knowledge and Processing of Risk Information and Beliefs about Personal Risk. Personality and Social Psychology Bulletin. 28. 836-846. 10.1177/0146167202289012.

21. Affirmations: https://www.sciencedirect.com/science/article/pii/S0897189723000216#s0060

22. Hand Model of the brain: https://drdansiegel.com/hand-model-of-the-brain/

Image source: https://atashajordan.com/cognitive-behavioural-therapy-triangle/

23. Kabat-Zinn, J. (2003). Mindfulness-based stress reduction (MBSR). Constructivism in the Human Sciences, 8(2), 73-107.

24. Sophie Su YR, Veeravagu A, Grant G. Neuroplasticity after Traumatic Brain Injury. In: Laskowitz D, Grant G, editors. Translational Research in Traumatic Brain Injury. Boca Raton (FL): CRCPress/Taylor and Francis Group; 2016. Chapter 8. Available from: https://www.ncbi.nlm.nih.gov/books/NBK326735/

25. Steven C. Cramer, Mriganka Sur, Bruce H. Dobkin, Charles O'Brien, Terence D. Sanger, John Q. Trojanowski, Judith M. Rumsey, Ramona Hicks, Judy Cameron, Daofen Chen, Wen G. Chen, Leonardo G. Cohen, Christopher deCharms, Charles J. Duffy, Guinevere F. Eden, Eberhard E. Fetz, Rosemarie Filart, Michelle Freund, Steven J. Grant, Suzanne Haber, Peter W. Kalivas, Bryan Kolb, Arthur F. Kramer, Minda Lynch, Helen S. Mayberg, Patrick S. McQuillen, Ralph Nitkin, Alvaro Pascual-Leone, Patricia Reuter-Lorenz, Nicholas Schiff, Anu Sharma, Lana Shekim, Michael Stryker, Edith V. Sullivan, Sophia Vinogradov, Harnessing neuroplasticity for clinical applications, Brain, Volume 134, Issue 6, June 2011, Pages 1591–1609, https://doi.org/10.1093/brain/awr039

26. Pittenger, C., & Duman, R.S. (2008). Stress, Depression, and Neuroplasticity: A Convergence of Mechanisms. Neuropsychopharmacology, 33, 88-109.

27. Singh B, Olds T, Curtis R, et al Effectiveness of physical activity interventions for improving depression, anxiety and distress: an overview of systematic reviews, British Journal of Sports Medicine 2023;57:1203-1209.

28. The underlying anatomical correlates of long-term meditation: Larger hippocampal and frontal volumes of gray matter by Eileen Luders, Arthur W. Toga, Natasha Lepore, and others. Published in NeuroImage in 2009,

29. Cascio CN, O'Donnell MB, Tinney FJ, et al. Self-affirmation activates brain systems associated with self-related processing and reward and is reinforced by future orientation. Soc Cogn Affect Neurosci. 2016;11(4):621-629. doi:10.1093/scan/nsv136

30. Koo, Minkyung & Algoe, Sara & Wilson, Timothy & Gilbert, Daniel. (2008). It's a Wonderful Life: Mentally Subtracting Positive Events Improves People's Affective States, Contrary to Their Affective Forecasts.

Journal of personality and social psychology. 95. 1217-24. 10.1037/a0013316.

31. Frijda NH. The laws of emotion. Am Psychol. 1988;43(5):349-358. doi:10.1037//0003-066x.43.5.349

32. Mindfulness Meditation and Resilience:

    - Davidson, R. J., & McEwen, B. S. (2012). Social influences on neuroplasticity: Stress and interventions to promote well-being. *Nature Neuroscience, 15*(5), 689-695.
    - Hölzel, B. K., Carmody, J., Vangel, M., Congleton, C., Yerramsetti, S. M., Gard, T., & Lazar, S. W. (2011). Mindfulness practice leads to increases in regional brain gray matter density. *Psychiatry Research: Neuroimaging, 191*(1), 36-43.

33. Learned Optimism:

    - Seligman, M. E. P. (2006). Learned Optimism: How to Change Your Mind and Your Life. Vintage.
    - Gillham, J. E., Reivich, K. J., & Seligman, M. E. P. (1999). Prevention of depressive symptoms in schoolchildren: Two-year follow-up. *Psychological Science, 10*(5), 461-468.

34. Exercise and Resilience:

    - Cotman, C. W., & Berchtold, N. C. (2002). Exercise: a behavioural intervention to enhance brain health and plasticity. *Trends in Neurosciences, 25*(6), 295-301.
    - Voss, M. W., Nagamatsu, L. S., Liu-Ambrose, T., & Kramer, A. F. (2011). Exercise, brain, and cognition across the life span. *Journal of Applied Physiology, 111*(5), 1505-1513.

35. Source for the "5 Whys" Technique:

    - Toyoda, S. (1930s). The original development of the "5 Whys" technique is attributed to Sakichi Toyoda, the founder of Toyota Industries. It was a part of the Toyota Production System (TPS) and aimed at identifying and addressing the root causes of problems in manufacturing.

- Ishikawa, K. (1985). Kaoru Ishikawa, a prominent quality management expert, formalized and popularized the technique in his writings on quality control. His work emphasized the application of the "5 Whys" in problem-solving and quality management.

36. Gerson, M. W., & Fernandez, N. (2013). PATH: A program to build resilience and thriving in undergraduates. Journal of Applied Social Psychology, 43(11), 2169-2184.

37. Alvord, M. K., & Grados, J. J. (2005). Enhancing resilience in children: A proactive approach. Professional psychology: research and practice, 36(3), 2383.

38. Höltge J, Mc Gee SL, Maercker A, Thoma MV. Steeling in Later Life: Exploring Age-Specific Effects of Varying Levels of Stress on Psychological Resilience. *Int J Aging Hum Dev*. 2021;92(2):170-196. doi:10.1177/0091415019871202

39. Gradual Exposure and Resilience: Cohen, S. (2004). "Social Relationships and Health."*American Psychologist*, 59(8), 676-684. This paper explores how social relationships and gradual exposure to stressors affect resilience and coping mechanisms. Cohen's work underscores the importance of manageable stressors in building resilience.

40. Micro-Doses of Challenge: Gillespie, B. M., Chaboyer, W., & Staltari, L. (2014). "The effectiveness of brief interventions to improve resilience and well-being in healthcare professionals." *International Journal of Nursing Studies*, 51(7), 978-988. This study discusses how small, manageable interventions and challenges can improve resilience and well-being in healthcare professionals, demonstrating the effectiveness of micro-doses of challenge.

41. Incremental Challenge and Stress Tolerance: Kubzansky, L. D., & Thurston, R. C. (2007). "Emotional Vitality and Incident Cardiovascular Events: Longitudinal Findings from the Women's Health Study." *Health Psychology*, 26(5), 644-652.This study explores how incremental challenges and positive emotional experiences contribute to resilience and overall health.

42. Psychological Theories on Stress and Resilience: Bonanno, G. A. (2004). "Loss, Trauma, and Human Resilience: Have We Underestimated the Human Capacity to Thrive After Extremely Aversive Events?" *American Psychologist*, 59(1), 20-28. This article reviews theories on how people adapt to stress and trauma through incremental challenges and resilient coping strategies.

43. Jamieson, J. P., Mendes, W. B., & Nock, M. K. (2012). "Improving acute stress responses: The power of reappraisal." *Biological Psychiatry*, 72(7), 579-585.

44. Neff, K. D., & Germer, C. K. (2013). *The Mindful Self-Compassion Workbook: A Proven Way to Accept Yourself, Build Inner Strength, and Thrive*. New York: The Guilford Press. This book provides a comprehensive overview of how self-compassion affects brain function and emotional well-being.

45. Lavis, M., Duggin, C., & Ross, J. (2020). "Self-Compassion and Cortisol Responses to Stress: A Systematic Review." *International Journal of Stress Management, 27*(3), 275-295. This study reviews how self-compassion impacts cortisol levels and stress responses.

46. Keng, S. L., Smoski, M. J., & Robillard, R. (2011). "Self-Compassion and Emotion Regulation: A Review of the Literature." *Journal of Behavioural Therapy and Experimental Psychiatry, 42*(4), 347-355. This article explores the link between self-compassion and emotional regulation.

47. Germer, C. K., & Neff, K. D. (2013). *Self-Compassion: The Proven Power of Being Kind to Yourself*. New York: William Morrow Paperbacks. This book provides insights into how self-compassion fosters resilience and affects brain function.

48. Limbic System and Emotional Processing:

- LeDoux, J. (2000). *Emotion Circuits in the Brain*. Annual Review of Neuroscience.
- Phelps, E. A. (2004). *The Human Amygdala and Awareness: Interactions Between Emotion and Cognition*. Proceedings of the Royal Society B: Biological Sciences.

49. Impact of Unresolved Emotional Issues:
    - Sbarra, D. A., & Hazan, C. (2008). Co-regulation, Dysregulation, Self-regulation: An Integrative Analysis and Application to Social Relationships. Association for Psychological Science.
    - Sapolsky, R. M. (2004). Why Zebras Don't Get Ulcers: The Acclaimed Guide to Stress, Stress-Related Diseases, and Coping. Henry Holt and Company.

50. Mindfulness and Emotional Awareness:
    - Kabat-Zinn, J. (2003). Mindfulness-Based Interventions in Context: Past, Present, and Future. Clinical Psychology: Science and Practice.
    - Baer, R. A. (2003). Mindfulness Training as a Clinical Intervention: A Conceptual and Empirical Review. Clinical Psychology: Science and Practice.

51. Chronic Stress and Health:
    - McEwen, B. S. (1998). *Stress, Adaptation, and Disease: Allostasis and Allostatic Load*. Annals of the New York Academy of Sciences.
    - Cohen, S., Janicki-Deverts, D., & Miller, G. E. (2007). *Psychological Stress and Disease*. JAMA.

52. Acceptance and commitment therapy:
    - Hayes, S. C., Strosahl, K. D., & Wilson, K. G. (2011). Acceptance and Commitment Therapy: The Process and Practice of Mindful Change. Guilford Press.
    - Harris, R. (2008). The Happiness Trap: How to Stop Struggling and Start Living. Trumpeter.

53. Incomplete Healing:
    - Enright, R. D., & Fitzgibbons, R. P. (2000). Forgiveness Therapy: An Empirical Guide for Resolving Anger and Restoring Hope. American Psychological Association.

- Worthington, E. L. Jr. (2006). Forgiveness and Reconciliation: Theory and Application. Routledge.

54. Persistent Distrust:

- Baumeister, R. F., Exline, J. J., & Sommer, K. L. (1998). "The Victim Role, Grudge Theory, and Two Dimensions of Forgiveness." Dimensions of forgiveness: Psychological research & theological perspectives. Templeton Press.

55. Emotional Baggage:

- Kornfield, J. (2008). The Art of Forgiveness, Lovingkindness, and Peace. Bantam.
- Tutu, D. M., & Tutu, M. (2014). The Book of Forgiving: The Fourfold Path for Healing Ourselves and Our World. HarperOne.

56. Negative Impact of Unforgiveness on Mental Health:

- Toussaint, L., Worthington, E. L. Jr., & Williams, D. R. (2015). Forgiveness and Health: Scientific Evidence and Theories Relating Forgiveness to Better Health. Springer.
- Harris, A. H., Thoresen, C. E., & McCullough, M. E. (2001). "Forgiveness, Unforgiveness, Health, and Disease." In The Handbook of Forgiveness, Routledge.
- McCullough, M. E., Pargament, K. I., & Thoresen, C. E. (2000). Forgiveness: Theory, Research, and Practice. Guilford Press.
- Smedes, L. B. (1984). Forgive and Forget: Healing the Hurts We Don't Deserve. HarperOne.
- Luskin, F. M. (2002). Forgive for Good: A Proven Prescription for Health and Happiness. HarperOne.
- Enright, R. D. (2001). Forgiveness Is a Choice: A Step-by-Step Process for Resolving Anger and Restoring Hope. American Psychological Association.
- Worthington, E. L. Jr. (2003). Forgiving and Reconciling: Bridges to Wholeness and Hope. InterVarsity Press.

- McCullough, M. E. (2001). "Forgiveness: Who Does It and How Do They Do It?" Current Directions in Psychological Science, 10(6), 194-197.

57. Forgiveness Misconception:

- Smedes, L. B. (1996). The Art of Forgiving: When You Need to Forgive and Don't Know How. Ballantine Books.

- Enright, R. D. (2012). The Forgiving Life: A Pathway to Overcoming Resentment and Creating a Legacy of Love. American Psychological Association.

58. Shonkoff, J., Levitt, P., Bunge, S., Cameron, J., Duncan, G., Fisher, P & Nelson, C. (2015). Supportive relationships and active skill-building strengthen the foundations of resilience. National Scientific Council on the Developing Child, 1

59. Affirmations and Virat Kohli: https://www.linkedin.com/pulse/how-virat-kohli-connected-stephen-r-covey-amit-garg/

www.ingramcontent.com/pod-product-compliance
Lightning Source LLC
LaVergne TN
LVHW061342080526
838199LV00093B/6919